WHAT PEOPLE ARE SAYING ABOUT *OUT OF THE CRACKS*

"As a psychotherapist, Expressive and Trauma Therapist, I was impressed reading Dr. Lasson's newest book as well as his first book of psychotherapy tales. In his work as a psychotherapist, Dr. Lasson allows himself to demonstrate the vulnerable side of therapists. Aside from describing some of his interesting client-therapist interactions, Dr. Lasson allows the reader to understand what might go through the mind of the therapist when dealing with challenging clients. Dr. Lasson's creativity, wisdom and his ability to intertwine Jewish wisdom in his work, resonates throughout the book and will benefit both therapists and anyone interested in the process of psychotherapy."

—Yehuda Bergman PhD. RDT, Expressive Therapist, Registered Drama Therapist, and Trauma Therapist in private practice, Baltimore, Maryland

"Dr. Lasson's keen insights into the therapeutic process, combined with his engaging storytelling abilities, make this book both an instructive glimpse into the world of therapy and a tantalizing narrative of human experience. Professional and lay readers alike will enjoy and learn from the extensive experience Dr. Lasson has to share."

—Raffi Bilek, LCSW-C, therapist, author, and speaker

"Once again, Dr. Jonathan Lasson has incorporated his clinical acumen, intellect, compassion and humor in his depiction of clients he has worked with over a twenty-five plus year career. *Out of the Cracks and Other Tales of Psychotherapy*, will be an ongoing source of inspiration for up-and-coming clinicians who deal with both challenging clients and those in severe psychological distress. Dr. Lasson demonstrates his vulnerability in describing his own conundrums as a therapist, which is rare to see in other written psychotherapy tales."

—Rabbi Dr. Tzvi Hersh Weinreb, Executive Vice President Emeritus, Orthodox Union; Editor-in-Chief, Koren Talmud Bavli; Author, *Person in the Parasha*

"At times informative, at times emotional, *Out of the Cracks and Other Tales of Psychotherapy* is a book that may draw tears. The stories within are told with a bare honesty that brings you into the room with Dr. Lasson as he navigates the challenging moments of giving people the help they need to do the best they can.

"Stories are the way that we communicate our deepest secrets, and our most cherished memories. Dr. Lasson excels at placing you in the moment, with an insightful psychological perspective on what is most important and most impactful. This is exactly what we need to gain a new paradigm to help us live our best life ever."

—Ari Gunzburg, Speaker, Coach, Wilderness Liaison, and Author of *The Little Book of Greatness*

OUT OF THE CRACKS

AND OTHER TALES OF PSYCHOTHERAPY

DR. JONATHAN M. LASSON

LEV AVOS PRESS
BALTIMORE, MARYLAND

Lev Avos Press
6210 Benhurst Road
Baltimore, Maryland 21209
doctorjonny.com

All names and identifying characteristics contained within the book content—including exact physical locations, occupations and other details—have been changed.

Cover design, interior layout design and project management by Ruth Schwartz, TheWonderlady.com

Ordering Information:
Quantity sales. Special discounts are available on quantity purchases by corporations, associations, and others. For details, contact the "Special Sales Department" at the address above.

Out of the Cracks and Other Tales of Psychotherapy /
Dr. Jonathan M. Lasson —1st ed.
978-0-9991309-3-3 hardcover edition
978-0-9991309-4-0 paperback edition
978-0-9991309-5-7 ebooks edition

Library of Congress Control Number: 2022915889

This book is dedicated in loving memory of my dear mother Greta Lasson who passed away on December 24, 2021. Every Friday night, our family pays tribute to the great women of our lives with a song called "Eishes Chayil" (Hebrew for "A Woman of Valor"). This one is for you, Mom.

TABLE OF CONTENTS

ABOUT THE BOOK TITLE
AND COVER DESIGN

The design for the cover of this book emerged from one of the tales included, but it was also inspired by a picture I saw of a small boy from an inner-city neighborhood bending over a small flower that was growing from the cracks in the pavement. The picture moved me greatly. And then I saw that scene play out in real life. I was working at a public school on Preston Street in Baltimore City when I witnessed a small child pluck a flower out of a crack on the street and hand it lovingly to his mother. It was Valentine's Day. I realized that even when the environment might appear dismal and cracking, there is always some new life budding forth. That is potential.

There are other reasons why Out of the Cracks was chosen for the title for this book. Recently a very influential rabbi passed away. His name was Rabbi Zechariah Wallerstein. Rabbi Wallerstein once wrote a brief thought about the inspiration he has when he visits the Western Wall in Jerusalem. I found this to be an apt depiction of the wall and how it relates to our imperfections as humans.

This is the thought of Rabbi Wallerstein. I have adapted it slightly for purposes of clarity, but the thought is his own and was one that helped inspire me to use "Out of the Cracks" as the title.

When you take a closer look at the (Kotel) wall (Western Wall of Jerusalem), it's full of cracks, plants growing in all directions, birds chirping all around. The most perfect place carries what seems like numerous imperfect qualities. In fact, the Kotel was the most "unimportant" wall of the whole Temple. And yet, G-d saved only what seemed to be unimportant—the imperfection. All those qualities are G-d showing us that his love is for the one who is not perfect. G-d has a special place in his heart for the person who struggles and therefore, his wall that he saved is exactly what it's supposed to look like! So, remember: you may feel like you are full of imperfections, but to G-d, you are the Kotel—the light in the darkness, the one thing worth saving under all circumstances. Your imperfection is the beauty. Your wounds and scars are the beauty. Your beauty is a reflection of all you have become. —Rabbi Wallerstein

INTRODUCTION

What a time these past two years have been! A global pandemic, mask-wearing, handwashing, social distancing, Zoom education, a country that has become more divided than I could ever recall, and for me personally, a time of tremendous milestones and accomplishments. In October of 2020, I became a grandfather for the first time to a beautiful baby girl. Five days later, and quite unexpectedly, I learned that I had become a grandfather for a second time. This time to a beautiful baby boy. Soon after, my second son got married and had a beautiful baby boy in November of 2021. Grandchild number three! In the summer, I achieved a long-awaited milestone of completing the seven-and-a-half-year cycle of Talmud study. This involved finishing one folio per day of intricate Judaic law and wisdom. This was my third attempt at this. Through persistence and the support of my wonderful family, I finally completed the study of the Talmud. These joyous occasions were mixed in with a broken wrist as the result of a softball game and the trauma of watching a parent decline. This is what we call life.

As of this writing, we are going through political turmoil and divisiveness. I am not a political aficionado. I don't follow politics

1

and do not engage in political discussions with people, especially family members. Politics has never really interested me. It is filled with negativity, bitterness, and divisiveness. I choose instead to read positive and uplifting stories or study the Talmud or other Judaic texts.

However, I did have a brief stint in "politics" that involved serving as president of a large shul (Yiddish for synagogue) in Baltimore. During that time, we were in the process of selecting a new rabbi, dealing with three lawsuits, and completing construction of our new building. I presided over countless meetings and used my psychological acumen and wit to diffuse arguments. People whom I had known for years suddenly became radicalized. I never heard so much yelling and bickering over such "important" topics as "We need to use Charmin toilet paper and not commercial grade toilet paper" and "I am offended that you decided to put the bulletin board right outside the bathroom! Now I feel self-conscious when I come out of the bathroom because it's obvious to everyone where I've been." I kid you not! To this day I laugh at how many gripes about the synagogue revolved around the bathroom. I was also internally dealing with the fact that I knew about many of the personal situations of the congregants, some because I was a therapist to a family member, or from other more direct interactions. I familiarized myself with how to run meetings. I verified what I had known for years: I do not like meetings. Finally, I came to realize that there is no business like "shul business." A synagogue, like a city or country, can become very political. The major difference is that you don't get paid to be president of a synagogue. Also, you are much less accessible when you are running a city or a country. At a synagogue you are right there in the pews without any security detail. I told someone after completing my two-year term that the best position to hold in a synagogue is one of *past* president.

The political climate has also revolutionized how therapy takes place. As a therapist, I have been confronted with clients who choose to talk about how bad so and so is instead of dealing with the fact that their marriages are falling apart, their children are becoming estranged, they have suicidal thoughts, or they're dealing with their own mortality. Such was the case with my client Helen.

Helen was dealing with stage 4 lung cancer and all she wanted to discuss during our sessions was Supreme Court nominees, climate change, and how bad America has become. She spoke from a place of pain. Her relationships had all deteriorated over time. It was unclear to me whether our sessions were a coping mechanism or whether they helped Helen take her mind off of her own suffering. She rarely had any visitors to her large home, and she had made no major breakthroughs in the four months we have worked together. She would frequently end sentences with the question, "Am I not right?" There is no correct response to that question—at least, if you want to retain that person as a client. With Helen, I have tried every trick in the book to divert the discussion to something more productive, but she always manages to find a news story to bring into the session. It seemed to me that her favorite thing to do in therapy is to show me a nasty meme on her cell phone that I believe is meant to make me laugh.

One session was a thirty-minute rant about a potential Supreme Court justice whom I knew absolutely nothing about other than her first name. I had a hard time following what exactly it was that Helen had against this person. She did state that she would lose her health insurance if "this Amy person" was appointed. I could not understand why she would lose her insurance, as she had VIP insurance, where her doctor saw very few patients and got paid very well to be at her beck and call. Her doctor, whom I have spoken with from time to time regarding Helen's psychotropic medications, seemed worn out by Helen but has continued to listen to her off-topic discussions about politics. Helen has the means to pay out of pocket for anything. An only child, Helen inherited a lot of money from her parents and has no problem telling everyone about her wealth. Although this further alienates her from potential friends, she persists in bragging about her extravagant lifestyle and ranting about politicians.

At some point during our time together, I made a deal with her that if she would not discuss politics for an entire session, the session would be on the house. I should have known that tactic would not work because she had no problem paying for sessions. I came to the realization that this was Helen's world of therapy. Other people would not listen to her; so she pays me to listen to her. As of this writing, I continue to see Helen. I am waiting for that breakthrough session. I don't know how this will end, but for the time being, Helen is comfortable with our weekly sessions.

Like my experience with Helen, the stories in this book are based on actual clients whom I work with or have worked with in my private practice, as well as in other work settings. As in my first book, *The Guilt Trap and Other Tales of Psychotherapy*, I wish to convey to the reader the challenges that therapists face when working with interesting, and sometimes challenging, people. The stories give you, the reader, a peek into others' lives, and they tell quite a bit about me as well. Though the experiences are true, I have altered identifying characteristics of each client to protect their privacy.

The Guilt Trap's success was partially due to its relevance. Readers found the stories relatable and not filled with technical jargon. People like to hear stories and are naturally curious to know what goes on in therapy. Those who have been in therapy report a variety of experiences, both positive and negative. In this book I share more stories to offer readers an additional look into the complexities of the human condition and how an outside-the-box approach can help develop creative ways to treat people who come for therapy.

Since the publication of *The Guilt Trap*, I have been asked by many readers how I have the patience to deal with other people's problems and help them navigate the intricacies of their relationships, insecurities, anxieties, and personality quirks. I don't have a simple answer to that question, yet I do believe that patience paid off in other situations such as when I served as president of a large synagogue, and it continues to pay off in my work as a therapist. I don't think all people can be taught patience, but I believe that active listening can be taught. Active listening and patience are different, in my opinion. Patient people are generally like that all the time. Active listening is a skill that can be taught and learned and sometimes even mastered.

Patience is not only a virtue, but also allows one the ability to think fast and think differently. For some reason, I thrive in stressful situations. However, I have come to realize that most people do better when calm. Last year I spoke with a family friend who was held up at gunpoint while backing out of her driveway. She told me that she would ordinarily have freaked out during that situation. Instead, she reacted calmly and with a resolve that she would not be carjacked that day. She put the car in reverse and sped away. I asked her if she was experiencing any trauma. She said that she wasn't and was quite surprised because she knew herself and how she typically reacted to even minor stressors. I believe she learned a lot about herself that day, and about how resilient she can really be under duress.

Recently, I took an online class (almost everything is online nowadays due to the COVID pandemic). The class was an eight-hour seminar on a particular method of therapy. I was struck by the rigidity of the approach. I saw the presenters wearing ties while discussing therapy. I cannot do that, and I don't think my clients would be receptive to someone who looks more like a lawyer than a psychologist. I have met psychologists, social workers, and other mental health professionals who like to be very directive and assign homework. That is not my style. I prefer a humanistic/existential approach. I have attended workshops where I question the efficacy of rigid approaches. I don't believe that people can unlearn dysfunctional patterns of behavior in ten to twelve sessions. There might be short-term relief, but therapy is a process that takes time and deliberation. My most successful clients are my most deliberate clients.

One reader asked me to give some tips as to how to do my brand of therapy. I am not usually fond of giving the "Seven Keys to a…" or "Five tips to a perfect…" (fill in the blank). I have been asked to write a weekly advice column: "Ask Dr. Jonathan." I graciously refused to do that because I don't believe you can adequately address an issue in a canned column that is edited to fit a space.

Instead, I would like to offer some ideas I have learned along my journey as a psychotherapist. At the end of the book, I will candidly speak to future therapists in the form of an "open letter to future therapists." The following ideas are for all readers.

1. **What is predictable is often preventable.** When a parent sits in front of me and time after time repeats the same thing—for example, "Billy and Bobby always fight

about who sits where on a car trip"—I have already developed my answer to the problem. What was the key word in the parent complaint about Billy and Bobby? The word "always." When a parent uses the word "always" it could be an exaggeration, but it often signifies a pattern. The idea I give is that if you can predict when Billy and Bobby will argue, lay down the rules an hour before embarking on the trip: "On the way there, Billy gets the front seat and on the way back Bobby gets the front seat." Again, if you can predict it, in most cases, you can prevent it.

2. **Families generally do not know much about each other.** People are, for the most part, very self-absorbed. They don't wake up in the morning thinking about other people, including family members. Conversations, if there are any, are short and superficial. For example, Marcia was complaining to me about how much weight her fourteen-year-old daughter had gained. She would constantly grate on her daughter's nerves by questioning her about what she ate that day. Obviously, this made matters worse. It was very predictable (see the previous idea). I asked Marcia about how her daughter was doing in school. Marcia could not name her daughter's friends (aside from two very thin ones, who were not really friends), and she did not know the names of a single one of her daughter's six teachers. My indirect advice was to get to know her daughter and stop staring at her waistline. Her husband thanked me for telling his wife what he had wanted to say for the past fifteen years.

3. **People are far more spiritual than they like to admit.** For too long, therapists have been ambivalent about

bringing up spiritual matters when, in reality, that is what their clients want. Rasheed had been in therapy for six months with his therapist Dr. Conrad. Rasheed would try to raise some existential issues such as the meaning of love; Dr. Conrad would try to give Rasheed homework on coming up with an "emotion wheel" to identify his feelings when he met someone who could be a potential long-term partner. Rasheed was more interested in "why" questions than how-to fixes. He wanted to explore the deeper meaning of life. Rasheed fired Dr. Conrad as his therapist.

4. **Families are not very adept at hiding their disharmony in public.** I always wondered why families fight in front of others. In one of my human observation binges, I watched families arguing, pointing angrily and looking apprehensive as onlookers slowly turned away. It is also interesting to watch families fight in their therapist's office. I mean...why drive to Dr. Lasson's office and pay him to watch you fight when you can do that in the comfort of your own home—for free? So families are like systems. You turn them on and watch them go. We can go back to the first idea. Families are very predictable. When Betsy rolls her eyes at her husband, Mark, you can predict with close to ninety-nine percent accuracy that he will have a negative reaction to Betsy's eye roll.

So once again, I give my readers a personal invitation to my therapy office. I share with you my private and intimate space of so many others who have shared with me their agony and personal stories, allowing themselves to become vulnerable with someone other than their close friends. I feel privileged to have gotten to know each and every one of my clients over the years.

My clients are dear to me. I have been criticized as foolish by one of my stiffer colleagues for admitting that I am actually fond of my clients. But I believe that fondness promotes growth and potential. Perhaps if more therapists became fond of their clients, they would achieve greater success. My clients are brave, and sometimes brash. They are often pained by life experiences beyond their control. But they delight in the glimpses of hope that emerge from the therapy room. Perhaps if we become more fond of them, they will reciprocate, and a therapeutic alliance can be achieved. I wish good things for everyone. May you all see prosperity in all facets of your life!

Fondly,

Your therapist

THERAPY ON THE FLY

There is a crack in everything.
That's how the light gets in.
—Leonard Cohen, Songwriter, in "Anthem"

When I was in graduate school, I remember I had a wonderful professor who taught me both psychopathology and how to deal with people in real-life crisis situations. Professor Cruz was a caring and compassionate man with a thick Cuban accent. During one particular class, students were assigned a specific disorder and asked to give an oral presentation about it, discussing advances in the treatment of the disorder. My topic was obsessive-compulsive disorder (OCD). I was selected to present first, but I didn't mind because public speaking has never really bothered me.

For my presentation, I spoke about religious OCD and over-scrupulosity. Over-scrupulosity refers to people who develop obsessions and compulsive behavior related to a religious ritual. They obsess to the point that it causes much anxiety, engaging in repetitive thoughts and behaviors related to that religious ritual. I recounted an anecdote about a former roommate who was always nervous when it came time to wash his hands. In Orthodox Judaism, people who are observant wash their hands before eating bread. Two times on each hand. This roommate was always nervous that he did not cover his entire hand with water, often spending several minutes washing his hands. It got to a point where his hands were so chapped from excessive washing that they frequently bled. After I finished discussing this case study, I spoke about therapeutic techniques and pharmacological interventions that were helpful in treating people who suffered from OCD. I was pretty satisfied with my presentation as I sat down to the light applause of my classmates.

Following my presentation, Professor Cruz called on the next student, Marcia, to give her presentation. I looked over at Marcia. Although I did not know her very well, I could see that she was trembling and was visibly uncomfortable. Professor Cruz came over to her desk and asked if she was okay. She shook her head to indicate that she was not okay. He asked her if she had a medical history, and she again shook her head, indicating that she did not. He then put his hand on her shoulder and calmly said, "Marcia, you are just having a little panic, and that is okay." He then pulled over a chair, engaged her in a worst-case scenario technique, and skillfully calmed her down.

This worst-case scenario technique—often used for people who are suffering anxiety—was employed to help Marcia realize that she would not die from a panic attack. Professor Cruz asked her what would happen if she had a panic attack in the middle of class. She responded that people might judge her differently. Then he asked what was the worst thing that could happen if people judged her differently. She responded that people would stay away from her. He continued, "What would be the worst-case scenario if people stayed away from you?" She responded that she would get depressed. "And what if you get depressed?" Dr. Cruz asked. She said she might commit suicide. "And what would be the worst-case scenario if you committed suicide?" At that point, Marcia smiled and realized that her thought process had become irrational.

As I watched Professor Cruz and Marcia, I questioned whether the whole thing had been planned in advance, staged as an example of the therapeutic technique. But it quickly became evident that Marcia was indeed having a panic attack. What my classmates and I watched was therapy on the fly. When Marcia was calm, she thanked Professor Cruz and explained that she gets very nervous when asked to speak in public. I remember that day like it was yesterday. I always wondered if I would ever have to do therapy on the spot like Professor Cruz had done.

Several years later, I no longer had to wonder. I had graduated with my Psy.D. (Doctor of Psychology) and was now on my own, working as a school psychologist while maintaining a private practice on the side. I truly enjoyed my job and was feeling very confident in my therapy skills. I also began teaching courses in psychology at several universities and discovered my love for teaching. Professor Cruz had been an inspiration for me to teach with passion, and I never forgot his in-class therapy with Marcia. It was now my turn to practice on the fly.

Although I've never had a student have a panic attack in class, there was one occasion where a student of mine had a seizure in the middle of class. I was teaching a human growth and development class to about twenty students. I can remember exactly where I was standing in the small lecture-style classroom. I was looking over my notes while the students were watching a short video on genetics. Suddenly, I noticed the student sitting in the second row—a quiet young lady who rarely spoke in class. Her eyes rolled toward the back of her head, and she was sliding off her chair. I was about to approach her when she regained her senses and sat up quietly. I told the class we were going to take a ten-minute break. As the students milled out of the room, a couple students who had seen her seize, stopped and asked if they could do anything. I asked them to stay in the room while I spoke to the young lady. I went over to her to ask how she was feeling; she seemed confused. I calmly informed her that she'd had a seizure during class and that I would like for her to go see the medical staff. Then I started asking her questions unrelated to anything medical. She seemed calm and insisted that she was fine, but I told her that I was concerned about her and that I would have these two students (who happened to be nursing students) escort her to the infirmary. After the class was finished, I made my way over to the infirmary and checked in on my student. She thanked me and said that she was not aware that she'd had a seizure. I told her that I would like for her to be seen by a neurologist for an assessment. That was my first experience with an in-class intervention. But over time, I have come to realize that as a therapist, I am always on call.

Back in 2004, I was on a family vacation in Miami Beach. My grandmother had been sick for a while. I was ambivalent about going on this vacation to begin with, but my family members insisted that I go because her condition could continue for several months and time with my wife and children was important too. Shortly after arriving in Miami, I received a call from my sister that my grandmother had passed away. I immediately arranged for a flight back to Baltimore to attend the funeral.

I boarded the plane and found my way to my seat in the back row—the only seats left because of my late ticket purchase. Seated next to me was an older woman who kept looking out the window and fidgeting with her purse. She seemed pretty nervous, so I did what came naturally to me. I asked her if she was okay. She told me that this was her first time flying alone on a plane, and she had a history of anxiety. I smiled and told her she had picked a good seat. She asked why. "Because I'm a therapist," I smiled.

Her name was Cora, and she was visibly panicking. I asked her to breathe along with me and follow my lead. She had a difficult time breathing, and when the plane encountered some turbulence, she reached over and grabbed my hand and squeezed really hard. I allowed her to continue squeezing as I tried a different tactic. I told her to squeeze her hands together in a fist for fifteen seconds and then relax them. We progressed to thirty seconds, and then forty-five seconds, and finally a full minute. As she was performing this technique known as progressive muscle relaxation, I told her to say the following: "Just like I can control how much tension I put in my body, I can control how much relaxation I put in my body." She continued with this mantra until she felt calm. She thanked me for the advice, smiled, and said, "I'm glad I was seated next to you."

It turned out that Cora had a history of anxiety related to a car accident she experienced about fifteen years prior to boarding that flight to Baltimore. She told me that she'd never gotten over the accident. A drunk driver had suddenly swerved into her lane, forcing Cora to smash into a parked car. The loss of control she had felt was unbearable. She never received therapy for this traumatic event and became terrified about driving, which generalized to flying. Any mode of transportation made her nervous—except for walking. She would panic whenever she felt this loss of control. Once again, I thought back to Professor Cruz's technique of worst-case scenario, but Cora was already calm and began telling me more about herself. (That's what happens when you're a good listener.)

Cora grew up without a father. Her home was located in West Baltimore on a street full of drug dealers and prostitutes. Her mother tried her best to provide for the family, often working multiple jobs, including prostitution. This meant that Cora was left alone at home to care for her younger siblings while her mother attempted to make more money so her children could have proper food, clothing, and shelter. This also meant that Cora was subject to harassment and sexual abuse from neighbors who frequented her home—and from her mother. Cora said that her mother was a good person and was just doing the best she knew from inner city street life. Cora's mother eventually found more gainful employment as a stock manager at a local grocery store. She saved up enough money to clean herself up and move out of their crime-infested neighborhood.

The family moved to a row home in a better part of Baltimore near a few universities. She enrolled in a couple of classes and saw that she had much more potential than anyone had ever given her credit for. She went on to get an AA degree and soon a bachelor's in liberal arts. Cora was proud of her mother. Despite her mother's newfound skills and interest in education, she was not well equipped for dealing with Cora's increasing level of anxiety. Therapy was never a consideration because among her family and community, therapy was strictly for "crazy people." Cora stared off and shook her head back and forth. "I wish I had therapy sooner."

"Do you think that you are crazy, Cora?" I asked.

"Oh, Lord Jesus, not at all!" was her reply. I said that was good to know.

Deciding on injecting a bit of humor, something I am want to do with my clients, I said, "And by the way, my name is not Lord Jesus. It's Jonathan." Cora let out a belly laugh, remaining calm for the rest of the flight. As we landed and parted ways, she mouthed a thank you to me. This was my first therapy on the fly. After this experience, I felt even more confident about my skills, especially with providing on-the-spot therapy. In fact, there have been numerous situations where my therapeutic acumen worked to my advantage—and to others who benefited from my skills.

My wife is a nurse. I work in mental health. Many people are of the belief that if you have a doctorate in psychology, it must also mean that you have extensive medical training. Although we are both in helping professions, my wife by far has more medical knowledge than I. Together we make a pretty good team when situations arise involving a possible medical/mental health crisis.

On another trip to Miami, we stayed at the Fontainebleau Hotel (before it had been renovated to less of a kid-friendly hotel). Our kids loved the lazy river, the many pools, and slides. The lifeguard had seen us for two consecutive days, and we had some great conversations. He was a gregarious man who worked for a company that employed lifeguards for this particular hotel. As we were resting on the lounge chairs, an acquaintance of mine, who I had not seen for a while, came over and greeted me. "Hey Dr. Lasson." Being that I am terrible with faces, I kindly asked him who he was, and he reminded me that he had taken a psychology class that I had offered. We talked for a bit and then went back to our families.

Suddenly, I heard the lifeguard screaming, "Hey Doc. Come here. Quick!" I looked behind me and then I realized that the 'doctor' he was referring to was me. I ran over to where he was and saw him kneeling over a teenage boy who was not moving.

When I got there, I took his pulse, which fortunately was strong. I asked someone to get a cold towel and some orange juice. He opened his eyes and seemed a bit disoriented. I asked him if he knew where his parents were, and he spoke in a mix of Russian and English. What I could make out was "Nyet." The person with the cold towel came back, and I put it on his forehead. Then someone else came back with some juice. I continued to ask him questions. Are you having a good time here? What has been your favorite place so far? He understood what I was asking and answered in broken English. He smiled at some of the things I was asking and seemed to be coming around. My wife came to my side and asked if there was anything she could do. By this time, the boy's parents came and with a worried look asked if their son was okay. I told them that he was likely overheated or dehydrated, and they should take him to see a doctor. They thanked me for my help. As we were leaving, the lifeguard also came by and thanked my wife and me. He then turned to my wife and said, "It must be nice to be married to a doctor." My wife nearly burst out laughing, knowing that the extent of my medical knowledge was a first aid/CPR course. This became a running joke in our family. Nowadays, whenever I am asked a medical question, my wife reminds me that it must be nice to be married to a nurse.

Sometimes my family members caution me not to ask random people how they are doing out of a fear that they might actually tell me how they are doing, which invariably turns into an hour-long, unpaid session. I try not to inconvenience my family with the "how are you doing" question, at least when we are doing something together as a family. While traveling by myself, however, sometimes I cannot resist having a conversation with a random person. It is just who I am. I enjoy talking to people, especially elderly people. I gain so much from the insightful, and often entertaining, anecdotes of others. As in every profession, there are always ethical considerations. Many professional development conferences and continuing education credits revolve around this theme. I have taught ethics in my role as a professor. Yet, I sometimes question the standards that are put in place. Although I recognize the need for an ethical code to protect the public and to keep psychologists in check and up to date with changes, I believe that for some clients, the codes can restrict clinicians from thinking outside the box. I, of course, follow ethical standards, but I do not plan to change my free style of operating. Thankfully, I have colleagues who are experts in ethics and deal with ethical dilemmas on a regular basis. I can always consult with them about tactics I use in the context of therapy.

However, there are some ethical considerations that those who set the standards don't quite grasp. For example, I live and work within an Orthodox Jewish community. There are many nuances that are specific to Orthodox Jews that seem foreign even to Jewish people who are not orthodox. For example, it is impossible for me to not see or interact with clients within our community. We see each other at synagogue, weddings, bar mitzvahs, brisses, and so many social situations. Rabbis regularly consult with those in the mental health community, and for the most part they are aware of the clients we work with. But, otherwise, our clients and their personal lives are confidential. Case in point. My wife became friendly with the wife of one of my clients. My wife, who does not know who my clients are, invited the couple over for a meal. What could I do? Tell my wife that this person's husband is a client of mine? Nope. Can't do that. So, we shared a meal together. At my home.

In the Orthodox Jewish community, there are Jewish laws that are unfamiliar to many non-orthodox clinicians. This sometimes creates a chasm between the clinician and the Orthodox Jewish client. What the non-orthodox clinician might see as abnormal or even psychotic might be perfectly normal in the Orthodox Jewish community. A non-orthodox therapist may misinterpret a client's behavior based on the therapist's own world view. The therapist may conclude that religious convictions are the cause of a client's anxiety or depression, but that may be an assumption and bias that doesn't apply to an Orthodox Jew.

My "whatever works" style has helped me out over my many years of practicing in the mental health field. I am flexible and able to shoot from the hip. Dr. Cruz was a great role model, as he had a very similar approach. He would not hesitate to respectfully call out a student or a psychologist who was too stuck in his ways. This was my style as well, even before meeting Dr. Cruz and watching him skillfully manage a student who was actively having a panic attack in class. When in stressful or unplanned situations, my "whatever works" approach comes in handy.

I also understand and appreciate that other clinicians have developed a more regimented method of practicing. I would even recommend them to a client who I thought would benefit from that type of approach. If it works for them...well, we respect each other for who we are. That's how I roll.

There is the old adage that you should not mix business with pleasure. But for me, my business is my pleasure. *Work* is something about which many people would say, When I get to know people, when I can be of help, I am learning and growing. It isn't work. It's truly my calling.

CHANGING
"HIS-STORY"

*One of the most sincere forms of respect is actually
listening to what another has to say.*
—Bryant McGill

W orking with criminals as a law enforcement professional takes guts. Working with criminals as a therapist takes grit. There are those people who work therapeutically with criminals who are criminals or ex-cons themselves. They understand each other. It is their culture. They share a spoken and unspoken language. As far as I know, I have never committed a crime other than a traffic violation and stealing a pack of baseball cards when I was twelve. I admit that I do not speak the same language, nor do I identify with the criminal culture. So maybe I am taking a leap here, but I view crime as an addiction. Once you commit a crime, you are committed to that crime. You own it. Whether or not you get caught, you know what you did. This is perhaps why we use the word "commit" when referring to crimes. Maybe that is why the stolen baseball card incident still reverberates in my guilty conscience.

As a therapist, I have seen the gamut of criminal behavior. Although I don't share the same culture, I work with the criminal the same way that I work with an addict. There is a lot of guilt in criminal behavior that resembles that of most addicts I have worked with. The first time, there is a slight fear of getting caught. If you get away with it, you have to up the ante. Although this may not be the case with crimes of passion, in cases where crime is for the thrill, you get to a point where you must make a life choice. Either drop it or accept that this is who you are.

How do I expect to make any headway with a criminal mind if I don't identify as one? The answer is that I never pretend that I am a criminal. I don't change the way I dress, speak, or act in front of a criminal who is in therapy. I show them the same respect I would show any of my clients. I understand that I am at a disadvantage in the therapeutic relationship right off the bat. These individuals did not choose to seek out my services. They were forced by the courts to come see me. So the walls are up. But that's okay with me. I am a very patient guy. I let them talk while I maintain a poker face. The only thing I do differently is I research the criminal mind.

Willie was no stranger to the legal system. Run a case search on him and sift through three pages worth of crimes from petty to serious and you would see all of his charges. Willie was referred to me by an attorney I was unfamiliar with, but I decided to take the case on contingency. (Attorneys have a way of pushing their agenda—even though it should be obvious to them that the therapist already knows their agenda.) The law firm of Jacob Tyson* was a smallish outfit of five criminal lawyers and a bunch of paralegals who were always looking to make their mark on society with that "big case." I see some of them in synagogue or at social events. This is their life. This is what they talk about nonstop. They can be pushy and manipulative at times, but that is perhaps what makes them effective at their jobs. They aren't my cup of tea. Maybe they have been hanging around the criminal element for too long.

When Willie came to my office, he was escorted by one of his lawyers, who sat in the waiting room. This is quite typical as lawyers act like coaches for the clients whom they represent. Before coming into my office, the lawyer looked at Willie sternly and said, "You better talk to Dr. Lasson. Don't just sit there and think that either I or he will help you." I escorted Willie into my office and offered him a water bottle, which he accepted. Willie was about six foot four and very much in shape. He had a swagger to him. He refused to make eye contact with me. I began with my usual questioning of "Do you know why you're here and what do you expect to gain from being here?"

Without looking up from the water bottle, Willie gave me the usual answer that I have heard too often: "You're gonna help get me off." I quickly corrected him by telling him that was his lawyer's job, not mine. With a look of frustration, Willie said, "This is bull."

After a few more expletives, he got up and was about to open the door when I said in a firm but calm voice, "I wouldn't leave if I were you." I guess I surprised him because he finally made eye contact with me.

"And why is that…sir?" I took note of his choice of the word "sir." It seemed obvious that Willie had ambivalent feelings about authority figures. I would address that later.

I continued, "If you were to leave right now, it would go down in my notes as 'Willie was uncooperative from the outset of therapy with Dr. Lasson.' You know where those notes go?" I let the words sink in.

Willie released his grip on the door and sat back down on the couch. "I didn't do nothing. They got nothing on me. Why do I need to go through this?"

"What makes you think you are different from anybody else I see?" I asked.

"I'm not crazy, and believe me, I know what crazy is," Willie responded.

"Tell me what crazy looks like," I probed.

At the onset of therapy, partial success is keeping a guarded person talking. Willie was obviously guarded and inhibited. This is the part of the process that I call collaboration. Willie and I were going to jointly explore what the word "crazy" meant.

"Dudes talking to themselves, saying crazy crap, you know. Picking their noses, skin, and stuff," Willie said.

I saw that Willie was ready for a little humor, so I said, "So you think those are the types of people I see here? Actually, the guy right before you picked his nose…always wiping it on the couch you're sitting on."

Willie let out a small laugh and tried to suppress it by coughing.

I smiled and said, "The people I typically see in this office are normal people with normal problems. You seem to think of yourself as normal."

Willie looked at me and asked, "Do you think I am normal?"

I responded, "I have only known you for about ten minutes. Do you think I can figure that out in such a short period of time?"

"Well, they say you're one of the best at this. If you can't figure me out in ten minutes, are you really that good?"

"How long does it usually take for you to figure people out?" My tone was casual. I was very happy that Willie was still talking. We were making progress.

"I can tell pretty quickly who is worth respecting...like in less than five minutes."

Now I could get back to my question about his ambivalence around authority figures.

"Respect," I said. "Respect," I repeated. "Let me ask you, Willie, in the ten minutes or so that we have been together, have I done anything disrespectful to you?"

"No. But I gotta meet with you for an hour a week. *He* told me," Willie said, nodding toward the door.

"Can you anticipate that over the time that we will be meeting, if you agree to return, that is, whether or not I will continue to show the respect I have shown you tonight?"

Willie paused and seemed lost in thought. Then he stared straight at me and said, "I really don't know who to trust anymore. Hell, I dunno if I trust those guys from the firm," he said, looking toward the door and nodding. "They seem like a fly-by-night outfit." Then he muttered under his breath, "Bunch of Jew lawyers." Without saying anything or needing to say anything, Willie held up his hands and said, "Wait, I am so sorry. I didn't mean that crap." I watched as Willie put his head in his hands. "I am so sorry," Willie said again.

"What are you most sorry about?" I asked.

Without missing a beat, Willie said, "You have not disrespected me since I have been here and you didn't deserve that."

"But Willie," I responded, "You were making a comment about the lawyers, not me."

"Yeah, but still. What I said was disrespectful to your people."

At this point in therapy, the therapist has a couple of options. Dig deeper or allow the patient to dig on his own. My impression of Willie was that he was capable of digging deeper on his own. I was convinced that there were people in his life whom he respected greatly, so I gave him a very pregnant pause. He took the bait.

"Throughout my childhood," Willie continued, "I always respected men who were disciplined. I thrived on consistency. I would work out every day and was very much into taking care of my body. My strength coach was a very influential man while I was in college." Again a pause. "I know. You're probably surprised I went to college. It was a football scholarship. I was on the O line at first and eventually Coach said I should try tight end. I did pretty good, but then personal issues got in the way. My dad cheated on my mom. She threw him out of the house, and my world turned to crap. I got into some serious drugs, and things changed."

Willie glanced up at me and continued, "I don't think I am a bad guy. I just made bad decisions and got used to making these bad decisions. What got me to your office was just being in the wrong place at the wrong time with the wrong type of cop. Yeah, I resisted arrest. It took about four of them to hold me back." Gazing at Willie, I imagined the scene playing out.

After a while, Willie looked at me and remarked, "You don't say much."

"I don't like to interrupt people when they are telling a personal story. I find it disrespectful," I explained.

Willie gave me a nod with a smile and continued. "Do you think it's possible that I was targeted because of my size?"

"It is certainly possible. People, especially those in positions of authority, assume that the biggest and loudest people are the main perpetrators." Again, I let that comment sink in.

"I didn't choose to become a criminal. I believe I was born this way."

"Willie," I responded. "You just told me that your world as you knew it came crumbling down after your father cheated on your mother. Were you born to have a father cheat on your mother? Let's say that never happened. Would you be sitting here today?"

Willie thought long and hard about this question. "The first time I got locked up, it was for possession of coke. It certainly wasn't the first time I did cocaine, but it was the first time I got caught. I was released after spending a night in lockup, which actually wasn't so bad. I was so tired, I fell asleep and the next thing I knew I was out on the street again. I figured that if I kept it to getting caught only once, and I was more careful in the future, I wouldn't get caught again."

"How did that work out for you?" I asked.

Willie let out a big laugh, shook his head, and said, "Got me here, Doc."

I was continuously thinking about his relationship with authority figures and decided on a different approach. "Willie, have you ever tried to contact your coach since college?" I asked.

"I saw him at Dick's Sporting Goods one morning after I got totally wasted, and I was too embarrassed to say hi."

"So, you do have a conscience!" I proclaimed.

"I guess," Willie begrudgingly admitted.

"Where is your coach now?" I asked.

"No clue."

"Have you thought about him?"

"Prison gives you lots of time to think. Coach was in and out of my life pretty quick. My dad *was* my life—until he screwed up."

"Tell me more about your dad."

"My dad, I think, or I should say I *thought*, was a good man. He went to church on Sundays. Came to every game I played. Planned amazing vacations. In general, he did lots of good dad things. But he was somewhat inflexible with his routine. Worked out every morning for an hour. Expected breakfast on the table after his shower and worked a regular nine-to-five job. Loved to take me and my brother to the shooting range. He was military. Not sure what happened to him while in the army. He didn't talk much about it."

"Did you ever ask?" I asked with sincere curiosity.

"Maybe once. I got the impression that it was not something he wanted to talk about, so I never pushed after that." I could see that Willie was processing something. "What was crazy is that the lady he cheated with sat in the pew in front of our family at church. Mom was pissed."

Reflecting back on Willie's case, I noticed the turning point in therapy came quicker than with other individuals who had been incarcerated and were coming to me involuntarily. Willie had a couple of things going for him. He was contemplative. He showed glimpses of a conscience. And it is possible, as he said, that his dad was in fact a good man, regardless of his mistakes. This would end up becoming a major talking point as we progressed in therapy.

After Willie initially attempted to leave my office and decided (wisely) to return, there was a certain change that came over him. Number one, he saw that he could not play me. Number two, perhaps he saw the good side of his father in me. And number three and perhaps most importantly, he saw that I respected him for who he was regardless of his extensive criminal record. This is something I have seen countless times in Willie's culture. They want and expect respect. Since Willie had felt disrespected often in his lifetime, respect was not something he longed for, it was something he expected of others. When a basic need, such as love, dignity, or respect, is taken away from someone, they feel entitled to have it back. In Willie's case, he had once known respect, but those expectations were temporarily eliminated when his father shattered that ideal. This idea was borne out in future sessions as Willie gained self-confidence while becoming less demanding.

As Willie was leaving the office that day, he gave me a firm handshake. Our eyes met. He nodded his head and walked out.

The following week, Willie indeed returned for another session. This does not always happen. I noticed as Willie came in and shook my hand that he was wearing a pretty nice watch. I hadn't noticed the watch at the first session. I commented on it.

"My Dad got it for me when I graduated high school. He told me that the two most powerful warriors are patience and time. I don't know where he got that line from."

"Tolstoy," I replied.

"You know a lot," Willie said.

"I read a lot," was my reply.

"I would love to read more. I just don't have the patience part. I do have the time!" Willie perked up when he said this, as if he had just said something very profound. I capitalized on this moment and gave Willie some homework. I asked him to read *Man's Search for Meaning* by Viktor Frankl. I loaned him one of the two copies I owned. He looked at the book and then laid it next to him on the couch.

Willie seemed a bit more chipper, so I let him lead.

"Ya know, Doc, I have been thinking since we first met; you mentioned the word 'respect' a few times. I took a walk after we met and asked myself why I deserve respect. I came up with physical stuff about myself and maybe linked to my dad's military lifestyle and lots of blame that I put on others as a reason for others to respect me. But they sounded like lame reasons to me. I could not concentrate on anything else for the rest of the day. I realized that I don't really understand the word. Can you help me out?"

"Well," I responded, "let me start by talking about your watch and what it may mean to you, consciously and possibly subconsciously. Watches obviously represent time. I have noticed that you respect time. It reminds me of a slogan that I heard from a mentor of mine. Early is on time. On time is late. And late is unacceptable."

"I like that," Willie said.

"Secondly, the watch symbolizes the good you saw in your father who gifted it to you with a message from Tolstoy. You saw your father as a mostly disciplined man with one obvious exception. He might have gotten that from the military, but, regardless, you respect both time and the man who taught you the importance of time. Now, where, may I ask, is your father and how much contact do you have with him?"

Willie hesitated for a moment and said, "He moved out to the Midwest somewhere and works in construction. He lives with a woman he met somewhere...probably at a bar. And in answer to your second question, I do not speak with him. He sends me a card every birthday and Christmas. It's been four years since I have actually spoken to him, though."

"I gather that you have lost a good deal of respect for him," I speculated.

"Wouldn't you, sir? I mean, c'mon man, he messed up. He showed no respect for my mom."

I looked at Willie and waited for him to process the strong emotion he was experiencing while speaking.

"That's what I mean by not knowing what respect is. I respected my coach but who knows if he's doing bad stuff," Willie continued.

I took a therapeutic leap that paid off. "And you respected your dad for a long time until he did some bad stuff. And I gather you once respected yourself until you got involved in some bad stuff."

At this point, Willie's six-foot-four frame seemed to shrink into the body of a child. With his hands covering his eyes, he put his head between his knees. The sobs were slow at first. Then they came in torrents. I came closer to him and rested my hand on his shoulder. He flinched at first and then relaxed. He realized I was not budging, and he was starting to realize that respect is not bound with perfection. It is not all or nothing. It is not black or white. It is not hero or zero. Respect is something that, despite our mistakes, we can regain.

After a few minutes, Willie looked up and accepted the tissues I was holding out for him.

"Willie," I continued, "I notice that your dad's lessons of respect are still with you."

Willie looked down at his timepiece and said, "Because of this damned watch?"

"No, because you are still calling me 'sir,'" I replied.

There are moments in the course of a therapist's career when we feel we facilitate a turning point. This was one of those moments. Willie was now contemplating his newfound understanding of respect. As I mentioned earlier on, I cannot fully appreciate the nature of the criminal, nor do I want to venture too far into the mind of a criminal. I have continued to research the criminal mind just to get a better understanding of how it works. I have learned that not all crimes fall into one category. There are crimes of passion, crimes of opportunity, and then there is the criminal who is simply out for the thrill. I did appreciate Willie's openness to change. Willie's case was for me one of those "pat yourself on the back" cases, where I was reminded why I chose this profession.

Over the next six months, I met regularly with Willie. Willie was essentially no longer obligated to come for therapy, as he had convinced me and the courts that he was interested in rehabilitation. He was now coming to sessions on his own accord because he wanted to. He saw the respect I afforded him and he, in turn, was respecting the process.

Another turning point was when Willie declared that he wanted to make peace with his father. During our sessions, Willie produced memory after memory of him and his father interacting in some meaningful way. He was now equipped with the tools necessary to begin the process of forgiveness.

I had prepped Willie as to how to handle this reunion and suggested that they go to a familiar place, perhaps one that had some sentiment for him and his father. Willie knew exactly where to go: the place where his father took him for his first beer.

Willie reported that the reunion with his father went very well. They met for about two hours, catching up where they had left off. As they took leave from one another, they hugged for a while, with his father uttering the magical words, "I love you, Junior." Willie said he had not heard those words in quite some time. They made a plan to meet up monthly. His father agreed to pay Willie's airfare to come to him.

As our final session winded down, Willie got up and said, "Sir, I want to thank you for everything you've done for me." We hugged briefly and said our goodbyes.

Willie's story is a story of acceptance and forgiveness. In order to begin the process of forgiving others, we need to forgive ourselves. I am sure there are many other Willies out there who have had negative experiences with authority figures. They tend to repeat the mistakes and create the history of an individual. Willie was willing to change "history"—by changing "his story."

BORDER CROSSINGS

*You can never cross the ocean until you have
the courage to lose sight of the shore.*
—Christopher Columbus

Early on in my career, it seemed like my supervisors always wanted to challenge me with difficult cases. In hindsight, I discovered...I was right. One of them admitted to me that she felt it was a good idea for me to see narcissists, although she did not provide me with much guidance as to how to deal with these cases. It was kind of sink or swim. As a rule of thumb, those clients suffering from personality disorders, such as narcissism and borderline issues, tend to be more difficult and time-consuming to work with than clients with other clinical disorders such as anxiety and depression. I had come to realize early on that my preference was to work with people suffering from anxiety in various forms. I found these individuals tend to be more motivated and likely to follow through on suggestions than those with personality disorders. Plus, clients with personality disorders may bring in more interpersonal dynamics, namely the dynamics between the therapist and client.

In *The Guilt Trap*, I recounted the story of a client who popped up at my front door. She tested the limits of the therapist-client relationship. After I discovered that she'd been "researching" my family members, I knew she had to be dealt with in a strategic manner. Jennifer was equally boundary-challenged but in a more subtle way. Many of the individuals I have worked with who fell under the personality disorder umbrella did not end up having successful outcomes. I've surmised that this could be due to my lack of understanding and my inability to be firm with clients at the outset of therapy. I feel that I have gotten better and have learned much about this population, but it still remains a challenge for me.

Jennifer was referred to me when I was an "emerging" psychologist. At the time, I was completing my dissertation and internship while at the same time juggling a family of three wonderful children and a move to a different city. But Jennifer's story sounded compelling, and I thought it should be straight-forward in terms of how I would approach the treatment. She was suffering from grief. Grief can be complex. There are layers upon layers that need to be peeled away in order to determine the source of the tears and sadness. I was familiar with grief therapy from running many groups for children and adults, even before my professional career began.

Jennifer's grief was multifaceted. She had lost her hair, her father, and her husband—all in one year. Jennifer had breast cancer. Her treatment caused her to lose her hair. She shared with me how she had had long blond hair and was grief-stricken over this loss. By the time I was seeing her, her hair had mostly grown back. However, she was self-conscious about her looks, so she chose to wear a wig until her hair had returned to its full, natural, healthy state.

Her father had suffered from lung complications due to emphysema. It was painful to watch as the dying process progressed. While her father was in hospice, Jennifer could not face him because of mixed feelings of anger, depression, and guilt. She was angry that her father had not taken better care of himself. He was a chain smoker and morbidly obese for most of Jennifer's life. Still, she had loved him for his intellect and his sharp sense of humor. She had many fond memories of her father regaling her with stories from the war and humorous anecdotes of his time working as a public school teacher. As his condition worsened, Jennifer stopped visiting her father and felt tremendous pangs of guilt as a result. Instead of using her guilt feelings to motivate her to do something pro-social, Jennifer sunk into a depression.

As her father was dying, Jennifer found out that her husband, Landon, an accomplished lawyer, was cheating on her. He would make excuses as to why he could not accompany Jennifer to her chemo treatments, explaining that he was in the middle of a very complicated legal case. In reality, he was meeting with a woman who lived in Baton Rouge where his firm had a satellite office. This woman was a paralegal with the firm. She was significantly younger than Landon and had lots of sexual energy, which fueled her obsession with Landon and Landon's for her. She also liked Landon because he was a very wealthy man. Jennifer found out about their affair from a family friend who used to work for Landon's firm and had seen the two together at a conference. After one seminar, this friend watched as the two pranced around together and later linked arm in arm as they walked into a hotel room. Jennifer's suspicions were confirmed after consulting with a private investigator who easily produced pictures of the two in various compromising positions.

Jennifer was beside herself. Landon apologized, but what hurt most was that this was all going on while she was suffering from cancer and undergoing chemotherapy. Landon assured her that the affair was over, but Jennifer was too hurt to ever consider taking him back. Jennifer, who always prided herself on keeping in good shape, could not imagine what would possess the man she once loved to engage in an extramarital affair.

Indeed, Jennifer was grieving on multiple levels. I strategized a plan to help Jennifer re-experience her grief in a way that would be therapeutic, rather than unnecessarily adding additional layers to it. I would ask Jennifer to recall positive memories of her father and what life was like before cancer. Although I was quite young at the time, I felt experienced enough to take the case. Grief was something I had come to know, although more so on the spiritual level than in the context of individual therapy. Helping others with grief was something I began doing at a relatively young age.

When I was in undergraduate school, I was looking for additional income. I found it in a very unlikely place. Next door to the school I attended was a funeral home. One day someone asked me if I could assist in preparing a body for a Jewish funeral. I had never done this before. I had never seen a dead body before. There was pay involved, which I accepted because I really needed the money, although I would have preferred performing this function for altruistic reasons. At the time, there was a shortage of people who wanted to do such work. Come to think of it, why would anyone want to wash a dead body, get it dressed, and prepare it for the coffin? But dead bodies did not seem to bother me for some reason. I performed this job for four years, and along the way I met with family members who wanted to know more about how we were caring for their deceased. I found that I was very good at listening to their specific concerns and educating them on the beauty in which Jews carry out the burial process. It is truly unique and extremely humbling. What I found myself doing was asking the family members to tell me something about the deceased. Since they were Jewish, the conversations usually centered around memories of meals shared for the Sabbath and holidays. We'd talk about their favorite foods, and I would always ask them about family favorite songs. Then I would sing one of the songs. I've always loved singing and have found music a great way to connect with people. Hearing those favorite songs almost always elicited tears—a healing salve for their grief.

I first met Jennifer on a hot summer afternoon at my office in Ft. Lauderdale, Florida. My office was located on Poinsettia Street in the posh area of Las Olas shopping district. I shared the office with an older psychologist, Dr. Charles, who was nearing retirement and slowly phasing out his existing clients. He was never there in the late afternoons, or on weeknights and weekends. I found that to be a convenient time to meet with my clients.

Jennifer was my five o'clock client and the last client of the day. While I was still with my four o'clock client, the sound of the chime on the front door told me someone had come into the office. Perhaps one of the other therapists was seeing a client or doing some paperwork. I did not give it too much thought. I was happy with where I was and was feeling pretty good that day. I always enjoyed going to this office because the decor matched my tastes: a distressed-looking wooden desk, a comfy couch, and some tasteful paintings of Ft. Lauderdale nightlife. Very simple.

At 4:50 p.m. I finished up with my client and went to get a drink of water near the waiting area. I noticed a woman in the waiting room who looked to be about thirty-five or so. She was wearing sunglasses, which seemed strange, as she must have been inside for some time. She also seemed annoyed, as evidenced by her flipping rapidly through the various magazines in the waiting room. I was unsure if she was there for me, so I asked her who she was looking for. She responded "Lasson." I tend to be very punctual with my clients; they generally will not have any wait time before their scheduled appointment. So, I was wondering why she seemed so annoyed if we still had a few minutes left before our scheduled session. I put it in the back of my mind with the intent of possibly addressing it during the session. I did not have to address it, though, because Jennifer took the lead.

Jennifer stood up and pranced into my office without acknowledging my greeting. Once she sat down on the couch, she stared at me and asked if I was usually this late starting my sessions. I gave her a confused look, to which she looked at her watch and said, "It's five o'clock already. My session was scheduled for four-thirty." I calmly explained that was not correct: "Jennifer, I am sorry if there was some sort of confusion, but I never schedule clients on the half hour. I only work on the hour."

"So, you're saying that I was early," she grumbled and slumped back on the couch. She then shook her head and began laughing. "I apologize. I thought I was over my chemo-brain. I totally thought my appointment was at four-thirty. I must have been thinking of my four-thirty hair appointment that, come to think of it, is actually tomorrow."

I assured her, "That's totally okay. I understand."

"I guess I did not make a good first impression," she continued. "I am not usually so grumpy."

I offered Jennifer a drink of water, and she gratefully accepted. "Are the lights too bright for you? You still have your sunglasses on."

"My eyes are very light sensitive. It was brighter in the waiting room," she explained.

She then removed her glasses, closed her eyes, and slowly opened them. I could see right away that she had been crying at some point. Her mascara had stained her otherwise very carefully groomed face. I offered her some tissues, and she dabbed her eyes. "Are you okay?" I asked, knowing that she was obviously not okay. The tears turned to sobs and there was a good deal of nose-blowing. I gave her a few minutes to regain her composure. I was somewhat used to this as that question typically opens the floodgates of tears or, at times, intense anger. I was okay with the former.

Once she settled down, she began with the usual unnecessary apology. "Sorry about that. I am overly emotional." I have always wondered why people apologize for crying in public. Logically, it does not make sense. You're sad. You cry. You're happy. You laugh. Go with your emotions. As time has progressed and I continue to see the inherent good in others, I have come to realize several things about human emotions. One is that people are generally uncomfortable showing their emotions publicly, especially if they are ones that elicit tears. They are essentially apologizing for something that should be normal, but they are not used to this kind of normal. I rarely hear people apologize for sneezing or screaming. Secondly, people are uncomfortable when they make others feel uncomfortable. When someone cries, it puts the listener in an awkward position. This might sound strange when the listener is a therapist. It's true that we are generally used to it, but still, it affects us in some ways. Thirdly, tears convey vulnerability and the desire to rescue that person from what is causing the somewhat healed wound to be reopened. Therapists often view this as progress or, in some cases, mistake the tears as a success on their part, instead of focusing on the client's feelings. I have watched many therapy sessions led by trained therapists. I notice that when their client cries during a session, there is a sense of satisfaction on the face of the therapist. It is very subtle but, if you watch closely, you will notice the expression that screams "Success!"

Jennifer had been playing with her hair during the session and reached into her purse to take out a mirror. After glancing at herself, she looked me straight in the eye. Jennifer's inadvertent mix-up of the appointment time seemed to be forgotten for the time being, and she asked my opinion of her hair. It was unclear to me at the time why, at that point in the process, Jennifer was so concerned about her appearance. Initially, I felt she was attempting to explain her mood at the time, which was...well...grumpy. Generally, I have a policy of not commenting on a woman's appearance, especially hair. It never seems to work out well. So I tried the therapeutic approach and asked her why she was asking for my opinion. She responded that she was generally happy with how her hair was growing in, but she wanted a man's opinion. This led to a discussion of why she wanted to impress a man. This was an easy one to figure out, as her husband had cheated on her. She was afraid that she had no longer been attractive in her husband's eyes leading up to the affair.

This line of questioning and reasoning can lead to transference and countertransference issues, as both the therapist and client are trying to achieve a level of understanding about the therapy relationship. As I have always said, therapy is a very intimate process. Clients expose their vulnerabilities to their therapists, and inexperienced therapists might take that as a cue to expose their own vulnerabilities. Thankfully, I was aware of this possibility and made a note to discuss it with my supervisor to receive guidance.

In Jennifer's case, I could have made a comment about her looks that would have steered the session in the wrong direction. That would have been counter-therapeutic. She accepted my redirection, but I continued to ponder the hair issue.

I remember reading one of noted psychiatrist Irv Yalom's stories about a client who wanted him to run his fingers through the stubble of the hair that was beginning to grow in following her cancer treatment and how much she appreciated his acquiescing to this request. At that point in my career, I was not as "outside the box" as I am now. I still remain cautious with certain requests, but I will double down on my feelings that outside-the-box approaches are far more therapeutic than cut and dried approaches.

After discussing the terms of confidentiality and having Jennifer fill out the necessary forms, she began to tell me what brought her in for the session. She proved to be an articulate and seemingly accurate historian as she detailed events in her life. She focused the last part of the session on her anger toward Landon and wanted to learn steps to get beyond her anger and move on. She stated that she had an ambivalent attitude toward men. On the one hand, she always enjoyed their company even more than she did women. She felt that men tended to listen to her better. This seemed a bit odd to me, but I tucked it away, knowing it would become "ripe fruit" for a future session.

The session ended in a somewhat uneventful manner. She looked at her watch and began to get up from the couch. She asked when she could schedule a follow-up appointment. I decided to take a slightly different tack with her request and said, "I would be happy to schedule a follow-up appointment. But I would like you to go home first and decide whether you feel I will be able to help you." She smiled and agreed to get back to me.

After she left the office, I took a stroll outside to think about the session. The sunglasses. The confusion with the times. My instinct was to give her the power to decide if I was the right therapist for her. The fresh Florida air and mélange of smells helped clear my mind; I concluded that it had been the right decision to put the ball in her court.

As therapists, we are often tempted to think of a diagnosis right after meeting with a client. I try to resist this temptation, but sometimes, I admit, I cannot help myself. She was coming to me supposedly for grief therapy, which I could handle. What I was not prepared for was what she really wanted out of therapy.

Later that night, I checked my messages and saw that Jennifer had called me almost an hour after our session had ended. She said that she felt I was the right therapist for her and that she was "very comfortable" with me, more than any of her past therapists. Perhaps I could have seen this as a yellow flag, but I was too tired to fully process the message.

Her next session was different from her first. There was no anger. She came at the right time, albeit fifteen minutes early, but this time she knew she was early. She was writing things down in a notebook when I came out to the waiting room to greet her. I made a mental note to ask her about what she was documenting in the notebook, which would eventually play a pivotal role in her therapy outcome. She looked up at me with a big smile and slowly removed her sunglasses. I couldn't help but notice her attire had changed. She was wearing a flowery sundress that may have been a little too revealing for a therapy session, but not that inappropriate for the Las Olas area. She was wearing makeup, but it was more tasteful than outlandish. She eased herself onto the sofa and looked up again, smiling as she arranged the decorative pillows in a way that would make her comfortable. I greeted her and decided to process her phone message with her before addressing her grief. "Jennifer, you mentioned that you felt more comfortable with me than with your previous therapists. I just wanted to explore that a bit. I also feel like it might be helpful for me to speak to your most recent therapist so I can pick up where you left off."

I was curious as to where this innocuous introduction to session number two would lead. Before responding to my question, she asked me if there was any way to make the lights dimmer, as her eyes were still very light sensitive. Without thinking, I immediately got up and dimmed the lights to a comfortable setting. I also do not enjoy a brightly lit office, so I did not see it as a problem.

She then addressed my question. "My previous therapist was helpless and meek. He wore a bowtie and made the sessions very formal and sterile. You seem more laid back and approachable."

This was not the first time I had heard about the approachable part of my personality, but that is just how I am. One of the people who inspired me to become a therapist was a camp nurse. I was working as a counselor at a sleep-away camp where she worked. I would typically hang out in her office, as she had one of the few cabins with an air conditioner. Being the husband of a nurse, I have learned that many kids who come to the nurse are not really feeling any physical pain but just want an excuse to get out of going to an activity they don't like, or they just need a little TLC. I found that it was usually the latter. This nurse, Mrs. K, was the type of nurse who really cared about the campers but would be overwhelmed by the numbers of campers who came to visit her. She could rarely take a break, so I would help her out with some of the minor cuts by bandaging them and sending the kids on their way. The other campers lingered for a while and would spend more time talking to the nurse. I found myself drawn to their conversations and offered to take them for walks around the beautiful campus. The nurse was always thankful for my ability to help her "triage" the campers. She commented on more than one occasion how approachable I was and how I would make a great therapist. Although I didn't need her compliments to keep me going, because I truly enjoyed helping her—and appreciated her air-conditioned facilities—it did feel good to get confirmation of what I already suspected. When I entered graduate school, I sent her a handwritten letter (which is what we did back then) thanking her for encouraging me to go into the field.

Jennifer's comment was nice and gave me the impression that she would be willing and motivated to deal with her grief issues. With the lights dimmed, I felt even more relaxed. I offered her some water, which she gladly accepted. Our conversation flowed freely with her telling me about her life and some of the challenges she faced in her marriage and her work as an ultrasound technician. She was no longer working and was no longer married. Instead, she was selling Mary Kay products from home and from her car, driving from appointment to appointment. She liked what she was doing, as she could make her own hours. This especially worked, as she could schedule fewer appointments if she was receiving any treatments or not feeling up to seeing people that day. I was curious to talk to her about the pain from her lost relationships. When I brought it up, she dismissed it, which was somewhat surprising at the time. I have realized since then that presenting problems is not necessarily the real reason people come to therapy. But this was still early in my career, so I naively thought that she really wanted—and needed—grief counseling, which I was really good at. When she dismissed the need for grief counseling, I began to wonder about her real motivation for coming to therapy. My concerns were exacerbated when I noticed her inching closer to where I was sitting. When she noticed me noticing this, she stated that sometimes she could not hear me because I was soft-spoken. Again, being naïve, I did not make much of this slight but purposeful gesture.

Jennifer returned to our discussion about her previous therapist and said she did not feel he could relate because of his sexual orientation, which she presumed was gay. She made a point to say that she had nothing against gay people, but because she was dealing with her husband's extramarital affair, she needed to see someone different. She then asked if I was married. When I told her that I was married, she did not seem fazed and asked me a couple more personal questions about my family and religion. The personal questions persisted a bit longer than I was comfortable with, so I redirected the conversation to her reason for coming to therapy.

"I just want to feel more validated as a person...as a woman." She let the words "as a woman" linger for a bit longer than necessary.

I am assuming the reader can see where this session was heading by now. However, as a young and naïve therapist, I did not recognize the pathological nature of what was happening. My sole purpose was to treat her for her grief, and I was stuck on that idea until the end of this session. As we were wrapping up, Jennifer restated that she really enjoyed the session and wanted to know if I do double sessions. My instinct was to say "no," but because she was booking the last session of the day, I said that I would consider it and get back to her.

I took a stroll around the block to process the session. I felt like I was making too much of her subtle nuances and that I should just concentrate on her treatment. However, I had a lingering feeling that she had ulterior motives for coming to therapy. I decided to place a call in to my supervisor. I left him a message saying that I needed to discuss this client before meeting with her again.

Since I had not heard back from my supervisor and wanted to get back to Jennifer and her request for a double session, I decided to call her and offer a onetime double session. Jennifer seemed very happy and stated that she wanted to really open up because she felt I was a safe person to speak to.

Admittedly, I was nervous about the next session since I had not heard from my supervisor. So, I talked it over with a colleague who told me that he regularly offers double sessions to those in need. I discussed with him my concerns, and he asked me how much of it was my own speculation. I told him it was more of a gut feeling because of Jennifer's dismissive attitude toward discussing her presenting problem. His response: "Jonathan, you should know from grad school that our clients' presenting problems are usually not their actual problems." I had heard this time and time again. He was right. "Maybe I am making more of a deal about this than I should," I conceded. Still, not hearing back from my supervisor was frustrating.

Although our next session was a double session, that did not prevent Jennifer from arriving early again. My client prior to Jennifer had canceled, so I decided to take her in early so I could get home at a reasonable time. When I came out to the waiting room to greet her, she immediately got up and walked toward me. Stopping a little too close for comfort, she said, "Thank you so much for agreeing to do the double session." She then proceeded to walk into the office and take her place on the sofa. I could not help but notice the perfume that she chose to wear that day. It was intense, and I immediately regretted agreeing to the double session idea. Her ulterior agenda was no longer my instinct. It was reality.

Jennifer sat and shifted positions a few times before beginning. To say that she was inappropriately dressed would be an understatement. I mustered up the strength and began: "So, Jennifer, what was the reason why you wanted this double session today?"

Again shifting positions, she deflected the question and asked, "Do you mind if I call you Jonathan?"

There are times in therapy where even the most seasoned therapists are confronted with questions that border on inappropriate. Clients with certain personality disorders may test the waters without thinking twice. They will blur the boundaries of therapy and friendship. At this early stage in my career—I was three months shy of completing my doctorate—I could not be called "Doctor Lasson" just yet. I decided to play it safe and said, "Most clients call me Mr. Jonathan or Mr. Lasson." Jennifer responded by saying, "I always liked the name Jonathan."

I took a little time to process this. "Why is that?" I asked.

"Well…I once had a crush on a guy named Jonathan. It was in high school. He was very cute. I think he also became a psychologist or a social worker. Something in mental health."

Deflecting again, I asked, "So, how do you think I can help you today?"

Jennifer was smiling coyly and explained, "I think I need validation. I feel so comfortable with you…I want you to validate me."

"What is it that you need me to validate?" I asked. I felt like I was sinking into a hole and was very unsure how to get this session on track. I also found myself becoming nauseous, which tends to happen when I am nervous. I did not want Jennifer to see that I was nervous.

"I need to feel validated as a woman. I have not felt validated in such a long time."

"Jennifer," I said with a slight croak in my voice, "why don't you start by telling me what happened with your husband and the affair? It seems like your need for validation as a woman might have something to do with the affair."

"Ya think!" she burst out laughing.

"Jennifer, I would really like to keep the session focused on the issues that brought you here. Can you assure me that you will do your best to stay focused?"

"Yes, Jonathan," she replied with a mischievous grin and some more laughter. "Where would you like me to start?"

I realized I was getting nowhere regarding her calling me by my first name. Jennifer was not going to cooperate on this point, and I felt powerless to change that. So I stuck with my questioning about her relationship with her now ex-husband and the affair.

"Why don't you start by telling me how you met and what made you decide to get married to Landon?"

"Okay, Jonathan," was her response. She was clearly enjoying this.

Therapy can be very tricky at times. Nowadays, when students ask me about entering the field, I am very cautious about recommending this career. I give them case scenarios of difficult individuals like Jennifer. I ask students how they would deal with such situations. Most students state that they would not have a problem with someone like Jennifer. Most of my students are female and they have difficulty relating to this type of situation where a female client is acting inappropriately with a male therapist. So I pose the scenario in the reverse, as it can certainly happen with a female therapist and male client.

Jennifer began her story. "Landon and I met at a party while we were both in college. Landon was simply dashing. We hit it off almost immediately. I sat there and listened as he would tell stories about the judge he was clerking for at the time. They were so funny he had me rolling. He would also tell me that he was out to make a name for himself in the legal world. He opened up to me about his strained relationship with his father whom he felt was messing up his own life. I liked that about Landon. He would share personal things about his life, and he was so captivating." Jennifer paused and asked, "Do you ever share stuff about yourself, Jonathan?"

I simply said, "Please continue," ignoring her question. I kind of felt like a lawyer at this point.

She continued, looking somewhat annoyed. "Anyway, Landon had a way with women, and I fell for him. He was into fitness, and we started working out at the same gym. We started seeing more of each other, and then one thing led to another. He assured me that I would never have to work, and he would give me a great life." At this point, Jennifer looked down at her feet and shook her head back and forth. "I can't believe I fell for him. I was young and hoping to find someone who was put together and would provide for me. When Garrett was born, our marriage seemed to head in a different direction. I was tired all the time and had a terrible pregnancy. I threw up a lot and Landon seemed disinterested in me as my body went through the changes that happen with being pregnant. One time, while I was pregnant, I planned a night away for us to reconnect as a couple. I planned everything to be just right, but then I started feeling sick again. So, Landon went down to the bar and did his thing."

"His thing?" I asked.

"You know…flirting with whoever would listen to him. He came back to the room in the middle of the night, and he was wasted. I was pissed, but I didn't say anything at the time. There I was stuck in the bathroom sick all night, and he leaves me to go and entertain himself with other women at the bar. But I did not forget about it. I still can't believe a man would do that to his young wife. I don't think you would ever do that with a significant other, Jonathan."

"Did you ever address it with him?" I asked, ignoring the personal aspect of what Jennifer was trying to insinuate.

"Yes. One night I had a drink or two and I told him what I thought of that night."

"Did you ever go for counseling?" I asked.

Jennifer laughed aloud. "Counseling? Landon never believed in it. He said that he knew from his friends that counseling ruined their relationships, but he said he was sorry and guaranteed that he would make it up to me. For the next few weeks, he became a model husband and future father. He would come with me to my appointments and shared an interest in setting up the baby's room. I actually believed that he changed. How stupid am I, Jonathan?"

"Jennifer. I don't believe you are stupid. You were in a relationship that you really wanted to work out. You had invested so much time, energy, and love into something, and you were willing to ignore these indiscretions, hoping for a life of bliss."

"Well, that feels very good to hear. You really are good at what you do. I am glad you think I am not stupid." After a brief pause, Jennifer continued, "So, when do you become a real doctor, Jonathan?"

I decided to answer this one. "In about three months I defend my dissertation. I hope I succeed and then I will have completed my internship hours. Then, I get the honor of that title."

"Are you excited?" she asked.

"It's been a nice journey. I really enjoyed school and learning about human behavior, especially the dynamics of relationships," I said, which probably sounded pretty silly.

"So, what is your dissertation gonna be about?" she asked, while shifting around on the couch.

I hesitated, but replied, "It is a program design. Basically, I am collecting data to create a premarital education program so couples can avoid pitfalls and learn effective communication prior to getting married."

"Wow! Sounds cool," Jennifer said. "I wish we had that. But as I said, Landon was not a believer and would never have come. Even if he would have, he would not have taken it seriously."

I was beginning to paint a mental picture of who this Landon guy was. Alpha male. Jock in school. Trying to prove to Daddy that he would be more successful. Not a committed family man. Father was possibly unfaithful as a husband. I quickly dismissed these thoughts and continued my line of questioning.

"Did you ever confide in anyone about your marriage and your suspicions about Landon?"

"Landon always put on a great show. We would host parties and he would be so complimentary of me. He would hold my hand and be warm and affectionate in front of others. After the parties were over, he would sometimes criticize what I was wearing and say I should have worn this or that. Or he would ask why I had said certain things. I never knew what he was talking about. I would ask for examples so I would get better at the party thing. He would just say, 'Forget about it.' It was always a letdown after a high point."

Our session was winding down. "I would like to explore more about the breakdown of your relationship, but I would also like for you to think of what you are hoping to get out of these sessions. Validation is important, but I think we should concentrate on objectives and long-term goals that you can move toward. You have lots of strengths and have been through a lot. So please think of what you would like to see as an outcome."

Jennifer stood up and said, "Okay, Jonathan. I will do my homework." She walked past me just a little too close. Then she looked back, smiled, and waved goodbye.

I sat down to write notes about that session, but I couldn't concentrate. There was no longer any question that Jennifer was playing me. I walked outside for about twenty minutes and then came back and decided to call a friend from my program and ask her advice. Julia had been a good friend throughout college and was a great listener. Although she was Catholic and I was Jewish, we were both religious, held strong values, and were happily married with kids. Julia was from Cuba and loved to share funny anecdotes about her family. She was very good at breaking down conversations into small, palatable points. I called her, and she answered right away.

I explained to Julia what was going on in my sessions with Jennifer. I asked her if I was making too much of Jennifer's poor boundaries, gestures, and attempts at redirection. Julia always seemed to know the right questions to ask. She was a great sounding board. I promised myself to always have someone to bounce ideas off, as it always helped me see things from a point of view that got me unstuck from whatever was causing me to obsess. Julia suggested that I pray for a successful outcome and the proper words would come. This was another thing I respected about Julia. She was one of very few of my colleagues who believed in the power of prayer and was not shy about suggesting that I say a prayer before my sessions. I began saying the "Doctor's Prayer" (a Hebrew prayer that some in the healing profession say) from that point on before I started my workday. It basically is a prayer that my interventions should be successful and to realize that healing ultimately comes with the help of a higher power.

The next session was going to be crucial. I was not sure how far Jennifer would push the envelope, but it came pretty quickly. She arrived early again for the next session. As soon as I entered the waiting room, she jumped up and said, "Hi Jonathan! I was so excited to see you today. I brought you coffee." Accepting gifts in therapy is an oft-discussed topic in ethics and psychotherapy articles. A coffee is not always an "unacceptable" gift, but you have to consider the context. I was a young, up-and-coming therapist who was not used to receiving gifts from clients. I was also unsure of how to deal with Jennifer, knowing that she was already pushing the boundaries. But I accepted the coffee and said, "Thanks, I appreciate it." There was no mistaking that Jennifer was dressing more provocatively. She took off her sunglasses and once again asked if I could dim the lights. When she'd first made the request, it seemed sensible given her past medical history. However, I could see how this request was driven by something other than her concern for her sensitive eyes.

The session began with Jennifer offering a compliment. I don't recall the exact words, but it had something to do with me being so young yet so capable for a novice therapist. Ordinarily, I would be flattered by the compliment, but this time my inner voice was telling me to be on guard.

The next thing that happened was even stranger. Jennifer continued to move closer to me while still sitting on the couch. Here I was already on guard, and she was inching closer. I inquired why. She responded that she was light sensitive and had trouble hearing me, and that she just wanted to feel close to someone. Then quickly, as if reading my mind, she added, "You know what I mean." It seemed like a plausible explanation, but I was not buying it. I think I understood her intentions. She was crossing a line.

Remembering the prayer that I had said prior to beginning our session, I took out a clipboard and asked Jennifer to write down three things she wanted to accomplish during this session and what her long-term goal was. She asked, "Why can't I just tell you?" I explained to her that it is more powerful to write it down because you become more committed to it. She did not write anything for the first couple of minutes, instead toying with the pen and looking at me for what seemed like an eternity. Finally, she wrote a couple of things down and turned over the clipboard, handing it to me in a deliberate manner. I read her words not expecting any bombshell responses. The first thing she wrote was "to feel validated by Jonathan." The second thing she wrote was "to explore my relationships." She did not write a third objective or a long-term goal. I looked it over again and said, "I see you left a couple of things out." She responded, "I can't really think of another one and I think it's too early for a long-term goal." I was silent, and she continued. "Besides, I really just want to get more comfortable with you (pause)...as my therapist. I don't really know too much about you."

I went out on a limb and asked her why she felt this was important. Her response seemed logical. "Well, as I explained, I got screwed over in my marriage and I don't like being screwed over." I asked whether anything had made her feel that would happen in therapy. "Absolutely not," was her response. "I do feel comfortable with you. In fact, very comfortable. But I like to know people. Like I now know you're married, although that doesn't seem to stop men from doing whatever the hell they want."

Self-disclosure is often effective as a tool during psychotherapy. I felt this would be important, not for the facilitation of understanding of her issues—rather it would help set things straight. "When we first began to work together, what made you think I was not married, Jennifer?" I asked. This question caught Jennifer off guard.

"Well...you looked so young for a therapist, and you were not wearing a wedding ring. So, I assumed you were not married."

I explained, "The reason I don't wear a wedding ring is for religious reasons. I am an Orthodox Jew, and many Orthodox Jewish men do not wear jewelry other than a watch."

Jennifer sunk back into the couch and said, "I never knew that. I guess I made the wrong assumption. In fact, I don't remember ever having met an Orthodox Jewish man before. That is so interesting. I guess I learned something new today."

The session began to take a different course; and I was happy about it. Jennifer began to stay focused on what brought her into therapy, and the focus on her therapist was put to the side. She sat in silence for a while and then started to become tearful. I offered her some tissues. She dabbed her eyes and sighed. I asked her where the tears were coming from. She said, "I am so desperate for a relationship with a man, and I need to feel validated as a woman."

"Why do you feel so desperate, Jennifer?" I asked.

"It's been a while since I had a meaningful relationship and Landon messed me up—up here (pointing to her head). He made me feel I was not pretty enough. First because of my pregnancy and then the cancer and mastectomy, I felt less feminine. I saw the change in him. When I was sick and not available to him sexually, he looked elsewhere to fill his desires. This made me feel objectified, as if I was only good for one thing." She paused and then added while looking down at her chest, "I did have breast reconstruction just in case you were wondering."

Jennifer was now making some progress. I chose my next words carefully. "I can fully understand your need for validation in an appropriate way. Your desire to try to get to know me better on a personal level is understandable because of how you perceive male-female relationships. I think that we should work on understanding the dynamics that led you to this point and come up with ideas that will help you make the right choices."

Silence. This was the therapeutic silence that integrated and outcome-oriented therapists crave. Therapeutic silence serves a couple of functions. It allows the client to process what was just exchanged during the session, either verbally or through gestures or body language. It also allows the therapist to plan the next move. Jennifer sat there and finally looked up at me. "Jonathan, I am so sorry for the way I acted and presented myself. I am so embarrassed. I admit that I might have been looking for something else when I came for therapy. I was more focused on our relationship than working to understand my own issues.

That still does not lessen my craving for male companionship, but I trust that you will help guide me before I mess up again."

My suspicions were correct although I did not share them with Jennifer. I had suspected that if she was willing to push the therapeutic envelope with me, she most certainly would have engaged in risky behaviors with men who were desperate and vulnerable. Instead, I just echoed her last word and formed it into a question. "Again?"

Jennifer looked up and said that after Landon, she would look for love in all the wrong places. She took out an ad in a local paper offering "companionship services" in the Ft. Lauderdale area. She said she had no shortage of customers. She liked the fact that men were paying her, as this served as a temporary validation of her womanhood.

Breakthrough sessions can bring amazing results in therapy. It took her inappropriate behavior to help her get to that point, but it was nonetheless very effective. She continued, "I have never shared that with anyone. Again, I am embarrassed and sorry for how I behaved here. I am committed to being more focused from now on."

I responded by telling her, "I understand your sense of shame, but I believe you are at least fifty percent over the hurdle." I learned this fifty percent over the hurdle technique from a former professor who taught us that clients need to know they are not lost causes. Some might say you are halfway over the hurdle once you make the first call for help.

I decided at that point to ask her if she wouldn't mind sharing her notebook with me. She eagerly took it out and showed me her diary of therapy. In it, there were many of her own self-reflections, which at the beginning were mostly negative. She added a rating scale at the end of each entry about how she felt therapy was going on a scale from 1 to 10. Toward the later stages of therapy, there were many more 7s, 8s, and 9s. I asked if I could borrow the notebook until the next session, and she readily agreed to this idea.

Jennifer and I worked together for the next few weeks. She came to recognize what triggered her strong need for male companionship and how to be more deliberate in her choices. She also came up with a list of what was most important in a relationship. By the time we finished therapy, Jennifer realized that what she needed in a man was someone from a stable family with solid values. She also recognized that she needed someone who, by virtue of just being together, made her into a better person. She defined what a better person would look like, and progress was deemed sufficient when we were able to taper down the sessions to just once a week. Between sessions, Jennifer would chronicle her automatic thoughts when she would meet a man and work through them in a more deliberate manner.

We also worked on self-affirmations of her feminine side. Each morning, she would wake up and stand before the mirror and compliment herself. She was also instructed to find some place to volunteer. I gave her this instruction to help take herself out of the self-absorption that consumed her. She chose an advocacy group for women and girls who had been in abusive relationships. She would spend a couple hours a week meeting with a young lady whom she would take out to a nail salon or to some other place where they could spend quality time together. Jennifer felt really good when she would come in each session and felt that she was finally doing something that would take her mind off her focus on herself. By giving, she was in fact, receiving. Suffice to say, she was appropriate during our sessions from that point on and remained focused on her goals.

As I was completing my internship and likely moving out of the Ft. Lauderdale area, I informed Jennifer that she would have to transition to a new therapist. She was initially upset at hearing this news, as we had developed a solid foundation for future growth. She was willing to continue to work on herself with guidance but was concerned that she would not find someone who would be ideal for her. She did seek my guidance on a couple of occasions after the termination of our therapy together. She informed me that she thought she had met that ideal man from a stable family with solid values. We spoke on the phone, and I felt more confident that Jennifer was headed in the right direction. After I moved, I heard from her one last time. For the first time, she called me by my new title—Doctor Lasson. I could sense she was smiling on the other end of the line as she moved on from her therapist—Jonathan.

As a young therapist, I was woefully unprepared for the likes of a Jennifer. Coming out of graduate school, it is tempting to diagnose disorders and say, "See, I was right." I try to avoid that desire to prove to myself my accuracy in being a diagnostician. With Jennifer, it would have been very tempting to classify her as an individual with a borderline personality disorder. There were a couple of factors that, in hindsight, would eliminate that diagnosis. For starters, there was her sense of self-awareness that she gained as sessions progressed. Secondly, she became responsible earlier than most individuals with this diagnosis. Thirdly, and perhaps most significantly, it was important to understand Jennifer in the proper context. She had an unconventional childhood and a relationship with her husband that was not well grounded in values and ideals, she suffered from cancer, and even with breast reconstruction she'd lost some of her self-confidence, which made her feel invalidated as a woman.

I therefore settled on a safer diagnosis of post-traumatic stress disorder, which seemed more plausible to Jennifer. My supervisor was pleased with this diagnosis and said that it would serve the two of us better in the long run than to make a tentative diagnosis of borderline personality disorder. There were indeed borderline features, but they were more situational in nature.

I thank Julia for reaffirming the idea that it is okay to pray for our success in treating our clients. Sometimes I surprise myself when the words chosen in therapy prove to be effective. I don't attribute the fact that the words come out correctly to my own skills. I thank God for that.

DAVID AND GOLIATH

*Leadership is not necessarily about
being the loudest in the room.*
—Jacinda Arden

Rashid was an unlikely person to become a client of mine. Rashid accidentally called me when he meant to call my father. This happens somewhat frequently as we are both mental health providers with the same last name practicing in the same zip code. Rashid was working as a police officer when he was involved in a high-speed chase that ended up with him crashing his police cruiser into an embankment and the bad guy getting away. Rashid was left with non-life-threatening injuries—and severe guilt. His attorney suggested that he go for therapy to help deal with some of the issues he was facing as a result of the accident.

When I clarified that my name was Jonathan and not Morris, Rashid asked me if I was taking new clients. I informed him that I was, but he clearly meant to call my father. At the time he called, the COVID vaccine had just rolled out. My father was not seeing anyone in person, but I let him know that I was doing in-person therapy. Rashid felt more comfortable with the in-person format than therapy over Zoom. After clearing it with my father, asking a couple of preliminary questions, and explaining how my practice works, Rashid agreed to an initial appointment.

Rashid came to my office on time for his first scheduled session. A slender African American man who appeared younger than his stated age of twenty-seven, Rashid looked like a deflated balloon. I learned long ago not to make assumptions about appearance prior to meeting a client for the first time, but I could not get over some of the features that distinguished Rashid from what you would envision of a police officer. Besides his slender appearance, Rashid did not walk with the typical swagger of a confident law enforcement professional or speak with any degree of confidence. He sported a teardrop tattoo on his neck and another tattoo with his mother's name and date of death on his left forearm. I could not imagine that the man standing in front of me had been on the force for very long.

Rashid took a seat on the couch and began by telling me that he had never been to a therapist before, but that he probably should have started therapy a long time ago. When I asked what had brought him to therapy now, aside from the insistence of his attorney who was working his workers' comp case, he stated, "Something is wrong with my brain." Curious to get a better grip on Rashid's issues, I wanted to immediately evaluate his neurocognitive abilities, as I was concerned that the car crash had caused some degree of brain damage. I referred him to a neurologist to rule out anything structural and went about my interview.

The interview went pretty well, all things considered. Rashid was a good historian. He remembered every school he attended, every teacher he had, every birthday party he celebrated, and all his family vacations. It certainly seemed like his long-term memory was intact. His short-term memory did not seem as sharp on first impression, but it did not seem significantly impaired, especially given the fact that he had just been in a serious accident. He explained that he was careless about locking up after he left his home, which was something new. I attributed this to possibly being depressed as opposed to a neurological deficit. I would later conduct a brief neuropsychological assessment on my own to rule out cognitive issues.

Rashid told me that he broke up with his girlfriend during COVID and that the social isolation due to the pandemic was "messing with his brain." Additionally, he lost his mother due to COVID-related complications. His mother had never been in good health. She and Rashid's father had been divorced for years, but they spoke regularly. Rashid thought it was probably good that they had split up. She suffered from diabetes and obesity and was a chain smoker most of her life. She had been upset with Rashid's career choice; she had expected him to choose a more "respectable career." She apparently saw the negative side of law enforcement, as Rashid explained, meaning hours away from home and alienation from the community. Rashid had always been interested in law enforcement. His father was a police officer and was currently, a district commander. His uncle was also in law enforcement but had recently died of a drug overdose. This further shed light on his mother's disappointment with his chosen career.

Rashid was dealing with lots of "stuff," to put it mildly. The stuff included the breakup with his girlfriend, multiple deaths, social isolation, and now a car crash that left him doing light administrative duties. His superiors decided that he would have to continue desk work until it was determined (by me) that he was fit to return to work.

Rashid confided that he wasn't sure whether he wanted to return to work as a police officer and was considering working as a security guard instead. At the time, morale among police officers was at an all-time low, with many officers being assaulted and the rallying cries across the nation to defund the police. Officers were dropping out of the force at alarming rates and crime was spiraling out of control in major U.S. cities.

Nonetheless, Rashid agreed to meet with the neurologist I recommended and to follow up for a neuropsychological assessment. He asked if he could still come for therapy while these tests were being conducted. I assured him that I would see him twice weekly for therapy.

During our second session together, we began with some relaxation techniques that included progressive muscle relaxation and deep breathing. Rashid admitted that he hadn't felt very motivated to come back for the second session. He did not think he would be able to relate to a white therapist, let alone a Jewish one, he explained. After our first visit, he informed his father that he was in therapy with a Jewish therapist.

Rashid's father told him not to judge the therapist based on skin color or religion. Then his father told him something about his past that Rashid had never known before. While growing up in the Deep South, his dad had been taken in by a kind rabbi. The rabbi employed him in the synagogue and allowed him temporary residence in a side room there while he tried to figure out a more permanent living arrangement. His father said it was the kindness of this rabbi that set him on the right path and saved him from a life on the street. Even after his father stole money from the charity box at the synagogue, the rabbi did not turn him in. Instead, he sat him down and read portions of the Bible about the importance of being honest in all aspects of life. The rabbi required him to work extra hours to pay off the money he'd stolen. Rashid's father said that, to this day, he visits the rabbi's grave every year to pray and thank him for his benevolence.

After Rashid's parents divorced, he had felt a little disconnected from his father. They reconnected when Rashid enrolled in the police academy. They would meet every Monday night to discuss police work and some aspects of Rashid's personal life.

His father had never been keen on Rashid's girlfriend and admitted that he was relieved when they broke up. His girlfriend did not seem very stable. Although street smart, her mood would switch on a dime. He thought Rashid could do much better. Later Rashid learned that his girlfriend was bipolar and that bipolar disorder ran in her family. He discovered that she was not taking her meds, nor was she faithful to him. Rashid was ready to move on to someone else.

The neurologist called me back a couple weeks later, informing me that there were no structural abnormalities noted on any of the scans. He sent me a report of his findings. We had already begun the neuropsychological assessment and so far, there was nothing out of the ordinary. Rashid had an IQ that placed him in the High Average classification of cognitive ability, with his nonverbal intellect far superior to his verbal intellect. He did very well on visual spatial reasoning and fluid reasoning tasks. Verbal abstract reasoning ability seemed to be his lone area of deficit. I then administered some psychiatric diagnostics and Rashid scored high in both anxiety and depression. I concluded that there was no neurocognitive damage resulting from the crash. The focus of our therapy would therefore center around treating his depression and anxiety.

At first, Rashid was doing well and was cooperating nicely with therapy and the "homework assignments" I gave him. Then things began to change. Rashid missed his next scheduled session. I called his cell, but he didn't return my call. I tried a few more times and the phone number was no longer in service. Since I had a signed release to speak with his attorney, I placed a phone call to the law firm. I finally received a call back from a young attorney who was loosely affiliated with the case. The attorney told me that Rashid had been admitted to a local hospital after he attempted suicide by swallowing about forty-five Xanax tablets. These pills had been prescribed by his primary care physician subsequent to his accident because he was having trouble sleeping. In our interview, Rashid had denied that he was taking any medications. This could have been partially true, as he never wanted to take them. He preferred to smoke a joint to help him sleep. Despite his apparent progress, clearly Rashid's depression had worsened—to the point of wanting to end his life.

It can be frustrating to watch a client who appeared to be making progress fall backward. I could not let Rashid just slip away. I visited Rashid at the hospital the next day. He was sleeping when I got there, so I waited a little while until he awoke.

I noticed a man in a police uniform approaching me. I assumed it was Rashid's father and stood up to greet him. He asked me if I was Dr. Lasson. I responded in the affirmative. He introduced himself as Rashid's father, Sean. He was a tall, muscular man, with a neatly trimmed mustache and a commanding presence. He had a deep voice, and what seemed to be a trained voice. I imagined that this man probably knew how to sing. He said he knew Rashid was seeing a Jewish therapist and assumed that I was that guy based on my skullcap, which I wore wherever I went. He understood that I could not talk with him about Rashid but wanted to thank me for helping his son out and that he would like to speak with me at some point if Rashid signed a release. I said I would be happy to do so if that were to happen. He sat back down in his seat and closed his eyes. I stepped out to the lobby to get a drink of water and return a couple messages.

When I returned to the waiting area, I found Rashid sitting next to his father. He was wearing a hospital gown that made him look even more slender than he already was. His eyes looked bloodshot. He was sniffling and holding onto some tissues. His father seemed to be doing most of the talking, nodding back and forth. Rashid noticed me standing there and motioned for me to come over. I patted him on the shoulder but did not say anything. At that time, there was nothing to say. I was there to listen. After a few minutes, he looked up at me and said, "I'm sorry, Doc. I don't know what I was thinking. I guess I am not right in the head." I told him to take his time and follow the treatment regimen prescribed by his doctors. I also informed him that the results of his brain scan were normal and there were thankfully no structural abnormalities. Then I asked him if he would be willing to allow me to speak with his father. He agreed and signed the release.

His father was an impressive man. He seemed to be the prototypical officer who was no nonsense when it came to understanding right versus wrong. He began by thanking me again for doing my best to help his son. He then told me what Rashid had already mentioned about the kind rabbi who helped get him back on the right path. He reiterated the deep appreciation he had for people of Jewish faith.

I asked him about Rashid's upbringing, and he admitted that one of his regrets was not being more present during Rashid's youth. He explained that his ex and he had never had an ideal relationship. Sean was into routine and physical fitness and his ex-wife did not seem interested in taking better care of herself. The divorce was somewhat expected as they drifted further and further apart. Together, they had three children. Desiree, Sean Jr., and Rashid. Desiree was happily married and working as a school nurse. Sean Jr. worked in social security, and Rashid, the youngest, chose the path of his father and uncle. Sean presented this information as if he had given it many times before. Sean seemed proud of all his children, but he added that he was always concerned about Rashid because he tended to make self-deprecating comments whenever he confronted failure. He also admitted that depression ran in the family, mainly on his ex-wife's side. He then asked me the question I'd expected him to ask: "Do you think he will ever be able to return to police work?"

I responded that fitness to work is somewhat subjective, but that I based my decisions on data and on how responsive the client is to therapy. Sean nodded and then looked downward. He seemed to be expecting that sort of response. After a minute or so of silence, I suggested to Sean, "Try to concentrate on spending as much time with Rashid as possible, make a time every week to meet, and be consistent." Rashid needed his father's presence, and I quoted him studies that show the efficacy rates of improvement from depressive symptoms when a father figure becomes a force in the life of the person suffering from depression. I told Sean that I would contact him and coach him how best to help motivate Rashid to continue with the therapy regimen. Then Sean asked me if I was a rabbi. I said I was not. He asked whether I was a religious man and if I prayed. "Yes," I replied. He then made a request, which I get from time to time: "Please pray for Rashid." I responded, "Of course."

Rashid was released from the hospital, and we resumed individual therapy. Rashid seemed more motivated than he had been prior to his hospitalization. He began speaking more about his father. He mentioned how he and his father were meeting up at least once a week. Rashid had also filled out forms to enroll in community college. This was somewhat unexpected, but Rashid wasn't sure whether he would be continuing in law enforcement and wanted to entertain other interests. The two classes he enrolled in were Introduction to Psychology and an English class. When asked about the psychology class, Rashid said that he wanted to become a victim advocate for those who were mentally injured from a crime. It sounded like a reasonable plan. He and his father had discussed the idea, and his father was proud that Rashid would be attending college.

In one of our sessions, Rashid informed me that he began having some issues with his vision. He had gone to the eye doctor earlier that month; his vision hadn't changed. (He had been wearing contact lenses during most sessions.) But he'd also been having nightmares that would wake him up and not allow him to fall back asleep. Additionally, he was having panic attacks during the day, which seemed to come out of nowhere. I explained that this is the case with most panic attacks and getting to the root of his anxiety would be helpful in treating the panic. Again, Rashid was very motivated to explore what was causing him so much anxiety that it was impacting his sleep and daily functioning.

I asked him if he would consider hypnotherapy. He admitted that he did not know much about this modality, so I explained the basics to him. He liked the idea that it did not involve pills or anything invasive, so we began with hypnosis during the following session. The first session, Rashid fell asleep within ten minutes. I allowed him the luxury of remaining asleep the entire session. I am a big believer that sleep deprivation causes much of the anxiety that people endure on a daily basis. I do not like waking people when I see them sleeping soundly. When the session time was about up, I gently nudged Rashid. "Was that hypnosis?" he asked. I told him that although falling asleep frequently happens, the hypnotherapy had not yet begun. I did advise him that he needed more sleep than he was currently getting. Rashid agreed that he was sleep deprived. I suggested that he come in for an additional session later that week.

When he came in for his next session, Rashid was smiling and seemed more relaxed. I asked him what was happening. He declared proudly, "I got an A on my first psychology test. I really like the class." He spent time actually reading the text—which came as a surprise to me. As a professor of psychology for over twenty years, I rarely had students who actually read the assigned textbook. Rashid, on the other hand, could not get enough of it and asked for recommendations for other reading material in the area of psychology. I said I would get back to him on that.

I asked him about the nightmares. He told me that much of the content of his nightmares involved buildings collapsing and crushing him, and he would have trouble breathing. "I remember Dad going into a church and rescuing a child from a building collapse. I could smell fire. I could hear people screaming and a baby crying. It was weird because it seemed like I was the baby that was crying. I felt a crushing feeling." We had to stop for a minute. Rashid's breathing had become labored. After he calmed down, he continued. "I saw a body that looked like it was burnt alive, but the lips were still moving." He then recalled a memory of hearing about how his father had rescued a child from a building collapse near his family home in West Baltimore. Although that building was not a church, it was situated next to a church. Rashid's family had moved out of West Baltimore years back and into a condominium in the Mt. Washington area of Northwest Baltimore.

During one of our hypnosis sessions, we processed Rashid's feelings about that building collapse. Rashid was able to articulate that he was facing peer pressure, which gave him this crushing feeling where there was no escape. The pressure came from friends who tried to get him to engage in negative activities such as drugs and street life. While he was under hypnosis, I asked Rashid to concentrate on the experience of the crushing sensation. He explained, "I feel like I am being pulled in different directions. My friends, who I can't really call friends anymore because they don't call me or want to be seen with me, seem to be hanging out with each other and doing bad stuff that I was trying to get away from."

"Go on," I encouraged.

"I sometimes feel like I can't catch my breath. I feel like my dad wants certain things from me. My friends are pissed at me because of my career. I just wish I could escape when I think about all this crap. I thought I knew what I wanted, but now I'm not so sure." Rashid started to tear up a little. "I wanna be tough like Dad, but sometimes I don't think I've got it in me." Because of his family history in law enforcement, this seemed to make sense. Rashid was facing an internal struggle with his friends who viewed law enforcement as the enemy. He said this was why they moved out of West Baltimore into a safer neighborhood where law enforcement was more appreciated. He acknowledged that as a teen he also experienced nightmares, but they went away when they moved. Now, he was once again hearing many negative things about law enforcement, especially after the George Floyd headline news. Despite being African American, Rashid's former buddies felt he was on the wrong side, and they distanced themselves from him. Rashid did not seem to mind so much, as he had made new friends in college. But from time to time he would still experience nightmares and anxiety, albeit far less in frequency and intensity.

While he was under hypnosis, Rashid was able to re-experience many negative events in his lifetime. He was able to process a particular time when he was being bullied by other students for wearing glasses. He would break his glasses on purpose to avoid having to wear them to school. His parents spoke with the school counselor about the bullying but didn't find the counselor to be very helpful. She had insisted that the bullying would remit as the boys matured. Rashid felt that this period of his life made him want to get in better physical shape to fend off the bullies. The sessions were producing nice results for Rashid, and his nightmares decreased and vision issues seemed to improve.

I asked Rashid about his feelings about returning to law enforcement. "I still think I enjoy aspects of law enforcement and I do enjoy that it gives me and Dad something to talk about. But I need to tell you, Doc, I am really liking the psychology stuff that I am learning. I wanna be able to help victims of crime and get to understand what they went through."

"Rashid," I said, "I am ready to fill out your fitness-to-work forms, but I want to be sure you are comfortable with me doing so." Rashid had made adequate progress since his suicide attempt and the department was waiting on his return if deemed fit. Rashid, under the influence of his father, had also begun to work out every morning and was in better shape than I had ever seen him.

"I am good with that. I do get some support from my officer friends and my dad. So, I think I am good."

At a time when the department was short more than a hundred officers, he would be welcomed back. I had Rashid complete some psychological assessments and his scores were good enough for him to return to work. However, Rashid wanted to wait until the semester was over.

"I would like to continue meeting with you if that's okay."

"It's not only okay, it's recommended," I said.

Rashid completed both classes and received an A in his psychology class and a B in his English class. He was satisfied with the results. His father was also proud, and they went out to celebrate. It was a wonderful evening and Rashid felt more connected with his father than ever before. His father, in turn, became more invested in the family. There were more family gatherings, and the family was happy to be back together.

As with many clients, just when things seem to be going well, there are some bumps along the way. Rashid had been progressing nicely and had enrolled in two more classes for the next semester. He was really enjoying the college experience and had developed a penchant for reading. In particular, he loved to read anything related to psychology. Rashid had also taken a part-time job as a security guard for a strip mall.

One night, as one of the stores was closing up, an employee asked Rashid to walk her to her car, as it was late. As they walked to the car, two armed men approached them. Seeing his security uniform, one of the men pistol-whipped Rashid and knocked him to the ground while the other grabbed the woman's purse. The last thing Rashid remembered was one of the assailants warning Rashid to stay away from the mall or he would get more than what he got that night. Rashid called his father from the lady's phone because he could not find his own. The paramedics arrived a short time later. Rashid initially refused treatment at the scene, but when his father got there, he insisted that he go to the hospital. He ended up needing seventeen stitches in his head. Rashid was not as bothered by the physical trauma as he was the emotional trauma. He felt he had let this woman down, someone who trusted him to protect her. He felt that he was also letting down his father and could not go back into any type of law enforcement.

I suggested a family session with him and his father to discuss his feelings more openly. The scheduled session occurred the following week. Rashid was dressed more casually than usual and came ten minutes earlier than his father. I suggested he should be up front about his wanting to leave law enforcement. I also suggested that we talk more about career plans going forward.

His father walked in and gave his son a quick embrace before taking his seat on the couch. His father was also dressed more casually, and I wondered if that was done purposely. I suggested that Rashid lead the session. Rashid agreed, took a deep breath, and began by saying, "Dad, I think I am done with law enforcement." His father looked downward and nodded his head in approval. He said, "Son, I was going to suggest the same. You did your best, but it is time you make decisions about your future on your own." Rashid breathed a sigh of relief and smiled. He then outlined a plan of action that included his ambitions to get his bachelor's degree in psychology. Rashid had saved up much of his money and was prepared to pay his own way through college, but his father would not hear of it. He insisted that he would pay and had, in fact, put away money for his children to go to school. Rashid was so excited that he jumped off the couch to hug his father. It was a warm moment where his father was able to say how proud he was of Rashid. Rashid was excited about college and beginning a new trajectory in life.

A change of scenery. Many of my clients simply need that change. It is a change not only in physical location but also a change in expectations or what is perceived as the expectations of others about them. There are always the parents who try to live vicariously through their children by choosing or gently convincing them to follow various career paths. Oftentimes, when I conduct an evaluation for work searches, I use questionnaires such as the Self-Directed Search to help guide clients toward the professions that match their personal characteristics as well as their abilities. Rashid scored highest on helping professions and, in particular, psychology.

As we reached our termination session where I felt that Rashid had achieved his optimal level of functioning, Sean asked if he could come in. Rashid was fine with the idea and curious to know why his father wanted to come in. I had a feeling about what this was about, but I let Sean do the talking. Once again, he was dressed in casual clothing, as opposed to his typical police uniform.

Rashid seemed to have his own agenda for the session, while his father had things he wanted to say as well. I began by asking Rashid how he felt he was doing overall and what he felt he had gained. Rashid declared, "I feel like I am able to think more clearly than ever. I take walks more often just to clear my mind. What seems clear to me is that I cannot continue with law enforcement the way I am now."

"What do you mean by that?" I asked.

"I don't feel I am cut out for this type of work based on what I've been through and how I reacted. I've just had enough and don't want to have to go through that again."

I looked over at his father, and he took a deep breath. Rashid's eyes were glued to a man he had come to admire with a full heart.

Sean started by saying, "Over the past few months, I have been doing a lot of thinking. I've thought about my career, the long periods of time I've spent away from the kids, and what I have accomplished till now. There is too much going on in law enforcement nowadays that is painting a negative picture about us. Morale sucks in the department, and I have decided it's time to begin the retirement process."

Rashid leaned into his dad and said, "But Dad, police work is your life. You are so good at what you do!"

Sean looked at Rashid. "I had a glorious career and can look back at some of my accomplishments. But as I look forward, I want to make up for lost time." It looked like Sean was going to choke up, but he cleared his throat and continued. "When your uncle died, I was devastated. My brother was gone, and I felt the world was spiraling out of control. About a week ago, I got a call from an attorney. He said that my brother had saved up lots of money over his career and had a business that I never even knew about. He left a good deal to me, and I would like to use that for what is most important in my life—my kids." Rashid and Sean smiled at each other and seemed to feel very relieved on multiple levels.

As they got up to leave, they thanked me for my help and then Sean presented me with a gift. He insisted that I open it. Wondering what it was, I unwrapped the ribbon from the box. It was a Star of David. Seeing my quizzical look, Sean said that the rabbi had given this star to him after he had stolen it from the rabbi years ago. The rabbi said that he should keep the Star of David as protection for himself and his family, as long as he promised to lead an honest man's life. "Being that I am not Jewish, and it would look strange for me to wear it, I have kept it in my drawer all these years. I want to gift it to you. I feel protected by the rabbi's spirit, and I think he would understand if I gave it to a Jewish brother." I was very touched by the gesture and thanked him for the gift. We said our goodbyes, and I sat back down in my chair and looked at the Star of David. I had just finished reading Malcolm Gladwell's *David and Goliath* and thought about how underdogs can defeat giants.

Rashid was certainly an underdog and felt this way much of his life. He was bullied in school, went through several traumatic experiences, but he demonstrated a sense of resilience to do what his heart told him to do.

Reflecting on this case, I thought about my role as a therapist. The night before, a friend had come over to me and said, "You don't pull any punches." I was wondering what he meant. He explained that he and his wife were both in the middle of reading my book, *The Guilt Trap*. He said he was surprised that I wrote about cases that did not always have a positive outcome or any known outcome at all. He continued by asking whatever happened to that guy in such-and-such a story. I told him that I had no clue. I try to follow my clients, but it is up to them to solicit my help if they choose to do so. Many times, I wonder what became of some of my clients, but I remind myself that my role is to guide them while they are with me. After they terminate therapy, I might pray for them, but I do not track them. This is what makes the field of psychology so fascinating. It allows our thoughts to linger, long after our work is done. Not knowing the outcome is very humbling. We do our best at the time. According to British psychotherapist Philippa Perry, "In order to stretch ourselves, we do need to experience the vulnerability of not knowing the outcome." As a therapist, I have learned to look at the counseling process as stretching ourselves and feeling vulnerable by the fact that our clients' stories do not end when therapy ends. Rashid's story has not ended. But I am satisfied knowing that this part of his life improved significantly. That alone is enough motivation for me as a therapist to continue to stretch myself in the work I do.

Starbucks Annie

*Whatever it is you're seeking, won't come
in the form you are expecting.*
—Haruki Morakami

I was sitting in Starbucks minding my business. My intention was to get some work done, answer a few emails, and write invoices for a couple clients. I noticed out of the corner of my eye that the woman next to me kept looking over at my computer. Sensitive to the confidential information on my laptop, I shifted slightly to ensure she could not see the screen. She continued to look over and I finally realized that she was not looking at my computer. Rather, she was looking over at a Hebrew book that I had been using as a resource for a talk I would be giving the following week. My talk was on the topic of resilience. My audience was a crowd of Orthodox Jews.

Finally, she asked me what the book was about. Going to a coffee shop is a fascinating experience. As a consumer of human behavior and caffeinated beverages, I am used to observing others in an environment that naturally lends itself to interesting conversations. Coffee shops should be an area of study in and of themselves. What is it about coffee shops that brings out a heightened sense of curiosity? Is it the coffee? Do coffee shop patrons have common personality traits? Why do people go to coffee shops to work? Do they really expect to get anything accomplished with the noise, and the curious customers? I came to the conclusion that coffee shops are a way of escaping the social isolation of drinking coffee at home. This is certainly not the case for all people who come for coffee. But there are those people who come to Starbucks to connect—either to Wi-Fi or to people. Annie was looking for connection. She found it in me.

This was not the only time a coffee shop customer eventually became a client of mine. The ethical codes are murky with regard to whom we can see as clients. As a fan of Irv Yalom's book, *The Gift of Therapy*, I, like Yalom, decry the stiffness that some therapists have when "misinterpreting" the ethical codes that govern the practice of psychology. Many articles have discussed the sense of rejection clients feel when their therapist does not respond to them in a "normal human fashion," but rather acts like a body showing early signs of rigor mortis.

Annie was in her mid-thirties when we had our coffee shop meeting over a Hebrew book. After realizing my time to myself at Starbucks was over, I gave in and indulged her curiosity about the book. I explained to her that the book was a commentary on the Book of Ruth. Ruth was a convert to Judaism who eventually became the progenitor to King David. Her resilience during her ordeal was to be part of my talk. I emphasized how strong Ruth was in the face of adversity and that she was a role model for resilience after loss of relationships and death. After hearing my thirty-second synopsis of the story of Ruth, Annie looked down and started to play nervously with her coffee cup. I noticed a tear in her eye. Stupidly, I remained "human" and asked her if she was okay. (I am not sure if my rigor mortis colleagues would have done the same, but I don't ever plan on giving up my humanity).

She then began to share that she was strongly considering a breakup.

In a relationship with the person she thought was "The One", Annie said that she had no strength or resilience. I took off my author's hat and transformed myself into the therapist. I said nothing but did lots of listening. It was getting late. She saw me looking at my watch and apologized. "I'm sorry for taking up so much of your time, and I hope your talk goes well." Before getting up, she asked me if I was a rabbi, to which I said "No!" She asked, "So what do you do?"

I informed her that I was a therapist. She nodded and asked for my contact information and if I was accepting new clients. I told her to call me, and we could discuss it over the phone.

As it turns out, Annie met Derrick whom she thought was "The One" at (you guessed it!) a coffee shop. Annie grew up in a rural part of Alabama but moved to the Northeast when she was young. Her father was a naval officer turned physician and her mother, a neonatal nurse. Neither parent was around much primarily due to their jobs but partially due to their personalities. Although they were married on paper, Annie described them as "casually married." They were both very independent and expected their two children to follow suit. Their marriage lasted for about eight years before they called it quits. Annie was six at the time and her younger brother, Alec, was four. They lived with their mother and saw their father occasionally. He was consistent only when it came to sending birthday cards and gifts that Annie said reflected her relationship with her father--- he had no clue what she was interested in. Eventually, he just sent money for birthdays. Annie's mother later told her that she and her father never had any major falling out. They just drifted apart. They had attempted to have a polyamorous relationship, including another woman for some degree of companionship. This woman was a very passive person who also wished to share in a relationship but maintain her independence as a freelance writer and traveler. Annie attempted to forge a relationship with her mother, but they did not see eye to eye on many issues, particularly when it came to politics and religion. Annie was far more conservative than her mother, and they often sparred over issues such as climate change and abortion. Eventually, Annie went off to college and became a criminal lawyer. She stated that she really did not like her job and had started looking for other business opportunities. Using her legal acumen and knowledge of policy, she became involved in a political campaign to help a struggling candidate attract more constituents. The candidate gained in popularity but fell just short of the votes necessary to unseat the incumbent congresswoman.

During this campaign, Annie would meet all sorts of people. Admittedly, she was also looking for love. She met Derrick while sitting at a Starbucks in Baltimore. She was immediately attracted to Derrick. His good looks and sense of confidence and similar political leanings drew them together. One thing led to another and before they knew it, they were dating on a regular basis and eventually moved in with each other at Annie's Fells Point apartment. They shared all living expenses and had very few disagreements about what was brought into the apartment, both in terms of style and friends. Since they generally agreed politically, they would host parties for like-minded people. Most of their friends were students from Johns Hopkins University. Their home became a popular gathering place, and they enjoyed playing the roles of host and hostess.

Annie and Derrick were very happy and began exploring the idea of marriage and family. Annie was desperate to move fast, as she feared she would lose what she described as her "baby-making abilities." Derrick was a bit more deliberate and wanted to have things planned out. Annie was more of the opinion that they should start a family as soon as possible and trusted that God would help them out. She did not believe in all this planning when "anything could happen" that could thwart their plans.

A week after a holiday party that they had hosted, Annie learned that she was pregnant. She was thrilled with the news but was unsure how to share the news with Derrick. She also wanted to wed immediately so they would be legally married before the baby was born. Derrick was surprisingly excited about the news and also agreed to a quick marriage at City Hall. Afterward they celebrated with friends and family and everything was looking great!

Baby Matthew, whom they called Matt, was born eight months later. Annie and Derrick were now parents, and both took time to dote over Matt. They made sure all his needs were met, and then some. They began to plan for Matt's education and realized that they had different ideas as to how Matt would be schooled. Annie wanted to send Matt to a private Catholic school and Derrick felt that Matt would do just fine in one of the public schools. Annie knew about the public schools in Baltimore from her work as an attorney. She became disgruntled when learning of cheating scandals, corruption at Baltimore City School's headquarters, also known as North Avenue, and lack of accountability for money that seemed to disappear every year. Elected officials seemed useless and often found themselves embroiled in scandals. Annie proposed the idea of a Catholic school that boasted rigorous academic and sports programs. She thought that by playing up the sports program, Derrick would agree. Initially, Derrick protested that sending Matt to a Catholic school would be cost-prohibitive. He finally agreed, however, after touring the school.

Annie and Derrick's marriage seemed to be going well. They would argue over only one thing: money. Derrick was fiscally conservative and did not believe in spending too much. Annie hadn't realized Derrick was so uptight about money, but this fact was becoming apparent. He felt they needed to save as much money as possible if they were to care for Matt and possibly other children. Annie insisted that they were in a good place financially and they should not worry about paying for school.

I asked Annie about her parents' approach to money. "My parents provided me with a comfortable childhood, but I never felt like they were really there for me," Annie explained during one of our first few sessions. "Money should never have been an issue. Dad was a successful surgeon, and Mom was a nurse turned stay-at-home mom." As successful as her father was, he did not spend much money on the family.

When Matt turned five, Annie and Derrick learned that they were expecting their second child. This threw Derrick into a pseudo tizzy fit. At the same time, Annie's mother told her that her father had been diagnosed with lymphoma and did not have much longer to live. The disease was attacking all major organs. Annie visited her father, but the visits were emotionally painful for Annie as she realized that she barely knew him. Compounding matters was the realization that Annie's children would never know their grandfather.

During our early sessions, Annie talked about her father. "My father was fully invested in his career. He would give presentations at conferences. He was an expert in orthopedic surgery and was sought after by many. He had written many scholarly articles and always seemed busy."

"I never really got to know my father on an emotional level. In fact, he was mostly devoid of emotions. He did gush when my younger brother was born and seemed to shower him with more attention than he did for me."

"Was that confusing for you?" I asked.

"In a sense. I was always the high achiever, and my brother was the slacker. I got straight A's and my brother was perfectly happy getting C's. Dad got him tutors, but Alec was very into sports and the dating scene. You would think that Dad would like the fact that I did so well academically because of his own strong drive."

"Tell me about how your parents related to each other," I asked.

Annie looked down and began wringing her hands. After a moment of reflection, her face contorted a bit, and she finally spoke. "I don't like to think about it too much."

I let the silence sit for a bit. After a while, Annie looked up at me and said, "Is that okay?"

I responded, "Annie, I would not have asked the question if I didn't think it would serve a purpose or have some relevance to your current situation. This seems like something you don't do very often, and I will not pressure you to tell me right away about things that are uncomfortable. But over my years as a therapist, I have learned that the things people don't like to think about tend to be very important."

"But it's in the past. Why do I have to bring it up? It's not like I can change them or my childhood," Annie responded, showing a bit more emotion.

"Annie," I said, "if your appendix ruptured in this office, what would you want me to do?"

"I would hope you would call an ambulance and get me to a hospital."

"And what would happen if I just sat here and stared at you writhing in pain?"

"I would think you were a cruel person," Annie said, giggling.

"And what would you hope they would do at the hospital that I couldn't do right here in this office?"

"Well, I would hope they would have the common sense to take out my bleeding appendix before I die," Annie responded, not sure where I was going with this Socratic questioning.

"Correct...I would not let you die. I would get you the proper help. You came to me for help. You considered yourself hurt. I would do what any good surgeon would do and remove your hard feelings, like a ruptured appendix, by having you purge them through talk therapy. Talking out your feelings can give you catharsis the same way you feel relief after a ruptured appendix is removed."

Annie nodded. "And how is this going to help me in dealing with Derrick?"

"Annie," I explained. "Therapy is a process. Your relationship seems to be related to past relationships that you have observed growing up. It seems like your script was faulty and filled with some degree of pain. I am going to help you rewrite your script with the hope that it will help you out with all future relationships."

Everyone has their own definition of failure. Annie's definition focused primarily on relationships. She really wanted to get it right. Annie was all about honesty. She wanted to have someone with whom she could be completely honest and transparent. She was very self-critical. She placed the blame of her failed relationships, both past and present, on her inability to communicate effectively. She was feeling a deep sense of shame.

From my perspective, Annie was a truly good person. She was not reckless and did not engage in many self-destructive behaviors. She was very faithful to her friends, family, and God. When I asked her what she was particularly ashamed of, she stated that she sometimes lied to Derrick about her whereabouts. Annie would tell Derrick that she needed to stay late at her office to work when, in reality she would lie down on her office couch and go to sleep. Annie had a difficult time sleeping at home and at the end of her day, she just did not feel like going home right after work. In her words, she needed time to decompress before having to deal with Derrick.

She asked me if she should tell Derrick about her "dirty little secret." I did not consider her after-work snoozing as a dirty little secret. I suggested instead that she address why she felt the need to avoid going home right away. "I don't like to confront people," she admitted, "and I don't want to have to deal with Derrick asking me questions about the credit card statements, which he always looks over with a fine-toothed comb." I challenged her on this based on her past work as a criminal lawyer with the intent that she would be able to differentiate between work and her relationship issues. Sure enough, this tactic proved successful. Annie stated that when she was working on a particular case, she transformed into an actress. Playing the "tough girl lawyer," as she called herself, and proving that she would persevere in that setting, was all part of an act. What she really wanted to do, was to become more successful in her relationships. This would become the focal point of our next few sessions.

During our fifth session, Annie expressed that she was struggling internally with our therapy. She confided in me that she could not understand why she could be so open and transparent with someone she had only met briefly, but not with Derrick. We discussed the concept of transference, which is very common in the therapeutic process. I cautioned her that my role was not to replace Derrick, but for her to redevelop her ability to be more open and expressive with Derrick.

Therapy can be a tricky field. Therapists who struggle with their own relationships should exercise caution when becoming enmeshed in their work with another person struggling with a relationship. Therapy can also be very intimate. As therapists, we learn a lot about our clients, especially when they feel comfortable in the relationship and begin to test the client-therapist relationship boundaries (coming early to sessions, calling in between sessions, and raising other red flags).

Thankfully, Annie did not have issues with boundaries. She understood my role as the therapist and her role as the client. The transference was more of her wanting a father figure to guide her through some of the trickier aspects of relationships. She did not have that in her own father and since she had mostly female teachers, she never really had a male role model to provide that type of guidance. She would mention from time to time how we had originally met and the story of Ruth and my talk on resilience. So, I decided to coach her on becoming more resilient.

Taking advantage of Annie's history of acting, I asked Annie to play the role of the therapist while I would act out certain scenarios that she could easily relate to. In our "theater class," we covered areas including confrontations over money, child-rearing, and dealing with end-of-life issues. Annie proved to be an excellent actress and "therapist." She played the role like an expert. When she would make a self-deprecating remark such as, "Well, Dr. Lasson, this is just acting. I can't do this in real life," I challenged her *cannot, would not, should not* vernacular.

For several weeks, we worked on her self-esteem, and she would quickly substitute her negative self-attributions with more positive self-statements. We would also play a word association game. I would say a word, and she would have to tell me the first thing that popped into her head, unedited. At first, her responses would be negative. I would say "Annie" and she would say "hopeless." I would say "tender" and she would say "mushy." As we progressed, when I would say "Annie" she would say "capable" and when I would say "tender," she would say "loving." I was very happy with this transformation.

Annie was becoming more communicative with Derrick, and things seemed to be going in the right direction—until Derrick was struck by a pickup truck while riding his bike. Derrick was badly injured and remained hospitalized for a few weeks before he was released. As a result of the accident, Derrick lost his ability to effectively communicate. Brain damage had caused aphasia.

Annie was beside herself. Just when things were looking up for her and her relationship, her husband had a near-death experience. Faced with the challenge of raising children alone, Annie informed me that she did not feel like she had the fortitude to withstand this obstacle. After many tears, I asked Annie if she remembered the story of Ruth. She nodded while wiping her eyes. Finally, she looked up and said one word: "Resilience." After a long pause, Annie continued. "Ruth had to deal with the death of her husband and the prospect of never having children, but she never gave up." Annie straightened herself, stood up, and said, "I can handle this, Dr. Lasson." I was very proud of Annie.

Unfortunately, Derrick did not make a complete recovery. His badly injured leg left him with a limp. Slowly, he worked up the energy to go back to work, but things seemed a bit different. Annie noticed a change in his personality. Derrick no longer commented on issues of money and was less of a high-strung person than he had been prior to the accident. He continued to be a doting father but was not the tense person he used to be. It reminded me of the movie "Regarding Henry." Henry, played by Richard Gere, had been a tough-guy lawyer until he was shot in the head in a botched robbery. With the help of a talented physical therapist, he recovered physically. But the most noticeable change from the incident was in his personality. With retrograde amnesia, Henry forgot much of his life before the shooting. When he was informed of the type of person he was prior to the shooting, he became disgusted by that personality and sought to make amends with those he hurt.

Derrick was not as narcissistic as Henry from the movie, but he was a difficult person to get along with at times. However, after the bike accident, Derrick was far more easygoing. Annie adapted to her new life with her "new" husband. The couple began a volunteer organization to help families of those who suffered from traumatic brain injuries. Their organization has made an enormous impact on many families. Both Annie and Derrick are very devoted to the cause. Annie spends many hours on the phone soliciting funds to help pay for medical expenses of those families she works with and is often tired, but she feels she is living a meaningful life. When she is super tired, you can always find her getting caffeinated at the nearest Starbucks.

Annie and I first met under a unique set of circumstances. A glance over at a book about a biblical character named Ruth and a conversation with someone who turned out to be a therapist and would eventually become her therapist seemed nothing short of serendipitous. Through therapy and her own strength of character, Annie now feels confident in her ability to meet life's challenges with fortitude and resilience.

OUT OF THE CRACKS

One small crack doesn't mean that you're broken.
It means that you were put to the test
and didn't fall apart.
—Linda Poindexter

Working as an intern usually affords those pursuing their degree in psychology the opportunity to benefit from different experiences. During one of my rotations in an outpatient facility, the interns were tasked with running groups for those who had been classified with a dual diagnosis. This meant that in addition to having a psychiatric disorder, the patients also had a substance abuse problem. This was not my favorite rotation for the dual reasons that I did not enjoy working with those who had extensive legal issues and that, at the time, I was the only male intern in the facility. Being the only male intern posed several challenges. One of the challenges was that I was generally called upon to respond to a fight or to a patient who was acting aggressively. The code that the hospital used to indicate that something was going down went something like this: "Dr. Strong. Please report to the A wing immediately." The assumption was that only males knew how to de-escalate aggression. Of course, this was certainly not true; the female interns were (at least) as capable as I was of calming down hostile people and averting a full-scale incident.

In this particular facility, the patients were exceptionally volatile and prone to outbursts, especially when they were deprived of their smoke breaks. We conducted mostly group sessions, but some of us were assigned patients to work with one on one. One of those patients was Rick. Nobody wanted to work with Rick. I reluctantly agreed to see him individually. I always enjoyed a challenge, but I honestly was not sure what I was getting myself into by accepting this assignment.

Rick was an ex-con who had been in prison for multiple DUIs, rape, and strong-armed robbery (robbery with intimidation, threats of force, or actual force). He was supposedly in recovery. I first met Rick during the second week of my rotation. Rick was a burly man in his late twenties, with many tattoos and a slight limp. He would always wear shorts, which, in itself was not remarkable because, after all, we were in Fort Lauderdale. But his shorts would always reveal his butt when he bent over—which he seemed to do quite often—and the image stayed with you longer than you'd like. It was unclear at first whether this was attention-seeking behavior or simply a guy who did not know how to shop for clothing that fit. I hoped it was the latter.

On one of the "Dr. Strong" calls, I hurried to a wing of the hospital next to the smoking section, a small patio near the inpatient unit. There was both an indoor and outdoor option for smoking. It's always nice to have options of where exactly you would like to annoy people. Apparently, Rick and another (much smaller) man were arguing, and it had led to punches being thrown. By the time I made it there, Rick was being held down by three male orderlies. One of the orderlies asked if I was from the outpatient unit. When I responded in the affirmative, he said, "Well then, this one is your problem."

I spoke to Rick in a soft voice and distracted him by asking him about a particular tattoo he sported on his neck. As a hospital rule, the outpatients were not supposed to mingle with the inpatients. On this particular day, Rick was on this wing because he had followed an attractive woman. When Rick saw something he liked, there was not much that could stop him. One of the other inpatient men tried to ward Rick off from this woman, and all hell broke loose.

I managed to convince Rick to come back to "our side" by asking him if I could eat lunch with him. Lunch was one of Rick's favorite activities, but he usually ended up eating alone. The cafeteria was situated close to the smoking section, and Rick would try to look for a woman to sit next to. Most people, especially the women, were disgusted by Rick. To put it bluntly, Rick ate like a pig.

Rick saw me coming over to his table and made some room. Having some company appeared to make him somewhat happy. As I got to know Rick, I learned that his eating etiquette was only one of his many non-endearing qualities. Rick also had a problem with flatulence. He loved to fart. He did not care where he was or whom he was with. Suffice to say, I did not offer to dine with him again when we parted after that first lunch. Thankfully, Rick ate quickly and my kind deed for the day was done. It was back to group work.

The group that I was to lead with was dubbed a "process psychotherapy group." Rick was assigned to my group. During this group, my co-therapist (another intern) and I were supposed to help our group "process" current content. Processing basically meant to ruminate over what was happening in the here and now. Although I am generally a quiet type of person, I have been known to become more animated when I am in a group. My co-therapist, Amy, was by far the quieter of the two of us, so I generally took the lead. I would present a topic and the group was supposed to comment on the topic. We would then ask group members to comment on the comments of fellow group members. Rick never held back. (His brain's executive function seemed to be dormant.) This would lead Rick to make inappropriate sexual comments to any female in the group, including the co-leader. Amy confided in me after our group that Rick was making her so uncomfortable that she wanted to leave. I encouraged her to remain and that we would process what she was feeling during our next group session. She sounded scared of that idea, so I promised that I would make the conversation generic and not point her out by name.

Rick reminded me of a patient in *Love's Executioner* by Irvin Yalom. In the chapter entitled "If Rape Were Legal," Yalom describes what can happen in a situation where one group member is acting inappropriately. The character, Carlos, who was dying of cancer, got into a heated exchange with a group leader when he asked personal questions related to her experience of being raped. Yalom brilliantly worked with Carlos in understanding how the world he was conjuring up would be problematic for Carlos' daughter if every man had a license to rape.

The next group I planned to try a similar tack and talk about how people were feeling in the group together. I was hoping that one of the female group members would speak up to take the pressure off Amy. Sure enough, Nicole, a young woman who was addicted to heroin in addition to having impulse control issues, was the first to speak in response to my question. "I think Rick is a 'perv' and he makes me uncomfortable." Rick had a huge smile on his face and seemed to enjoy the fact that he was being called out.

Amy shifted in her chair, and I took the cue from her. "Rick, how would you like to respond to Nicole?"

Without batting an eyelash, Rick stated, "Look at what Nicole's wearing today. She obviously wants something."

"Rick," I said, "is it possible for you to imagine that you are making some people uncomfortable?"

"Yes," Rick replied. "Amy over there looks like she's squirming. I would love to make her squirm even more." I could see that Amy was about to lose it, so I gave her a look that told her to calm down.

"Well Rick, as a guy and as an onlooker to this process, I am sensing a lot of discomfort from the women in the group because of the way you are talking. I know you have been through some stuff. Maybe you would like to share with the group what you have experienced in your life that would make you enjoy causing other people, especially women, all of this 'squirminess'?"

Amy relaxed a little bit, as she realized I was taking over as the group facilitator for the time being. Rick was also a bit disarmed by my presentation. Rick replied, "Already went over this with my therapist. Why do I need to share it with these people I barely know?"

I began, "Rick, everyone in this room has a story. Most of them are probably painful. My job is to help process these stories together with the group so that we can come to a better understanding of each other and begin to respect each other's preferences and differences. I don't want you to respond to what I just said. Just think about it and meet me after tomorrow morning's group." I purposely wanted to postpone his response until we had the chance for another lunch meeting. Even though

I had quietly vowed never to eat with him again, I was on a mission to rehab Rick.

The next day, Rick picked up his food, and I brought my PB&J sandwich over to the small round table where Rick usually plopped himself down. We first talked about basketball. He was a Miami Heat fan, and the Heat were doing pretty well that season. His favorite player was Tim Hardaway. Rick seemed to love saying his name. Go figure.

My love for the game of basketball gave us something to speak about. Of course, Rick liked to talk about the cheerleaders. It seemed that for Rick, all discussions had to have a sexual component in order to qualify as conversation. I made a mental note to address this.

First though, I wanted to address his etiquette while eating. I told Rick that if he wanted to become more endearing to others (which to him meant all the women in the group), he would have to work on his eating habits. I gave him a lesson on how to bring the food to his mouth as opposed to bringing his mouth to the food. This took a while for him to master. Next, we talked about eating a little slower. I then put him to a challenge. If he were to get better with his eating etiquette for one week, I would give him extended smoke breaks. If he improved his language, I would give him a Tim Hardaway rookie card. A couple years before this internship, I taught a sixth-grade class at a local private school. At the end of the school year, one of my students gave me a gift of basketball cards, that included the Hardaway card. Rick was up for the challenge. I was quietly satisfied with myself that I was able to make deals that would not cost me much but would help accomplish my goal for a patient.

Over the course of our lunch conversations, Rick told me a little more about his childhood and particular experiences that had led him down the path he had taken, starting from the time he was twelve years old. It was for this reason I believed I was making some headway in rehabbing Rick. I had kept him talking. Growing up with an alcoholic dad who made promises that were never fulfilled, Rick developed a distrust for males in a position of authority. His father would often promise to take Rick to sporting events. But his father would never show up. Nor did his father show up to anything that had to do with Rick's schooling.

Rick saw me as a consistent male in a position with minimal authority. Every promise I made to Rick, I stuck by. Rick got his extended smoke breaks and his Tim Hardaway card. I gave Rick constant praise, and he seemed to be taking a liking to my style. Although I was not yet a doctor, he insisted on calling me "Doc." He said I was the only person he felt comfortable talking to. I learned early on that as easy as it was to dislike a person like Rick, it was not hard to find some admirable qualities as well. For example, Rick was very blunt. While his directness may have come off as rude to many, I saw it as him just being honest about how he felt. Obviously, his style needed some tweaking, but his honesty was an admirable trait. And Rick showed confidence and passion about the things he liked. Yes, his repertoire in this area was limited to mostly inappropriate topics, but his enthusiasm was remarkable.

Rick shared with me more about his life, including his father's extensive porn collection and his womanizing behaviors. Rick had met his first girlfriend in seventh grade. Rick's knowledge of how to treat a girl was learned primarily from his father, who was not a highly effective teacher. His mother was not much better. Rick objectified his first girlfriend and attempted to "get into her pants" (in his words) pretty soon into the relationship.

She was not ready for sexual activity, and in reaction Rick became angry and verbally abusive toward her. She informed the counselor at school and Rick's parents were called in for a meeting. Rick was subsequently expelled from school for this behavior. Rick did not last long at any one school. He ended up dropping out of school in ninth grade and dropping into the juvenile system at age fifteen.

Rick's mother was an addict who would sell her body for drugs. Prior to her addiction, she had attempted some college. She was a bright woman with much promise. Rick stated that she could have been a lawyer, but she chose the "oldest profession" instead. Many men passed through his house, and on more than one occasion, he watched his mother engaging in various sexual acts with random men for pay. Rick told me how he often pleasured himself to images of his mother, and this brought a certain level of shame when he was young. As time went by, he said he did not have much of a conscience and believed that his behavior was entirely normal.

When I returned to the group for the next session, Rick was not present. Apparently, according to the secretary, he was feeling under the weather. During the group, members did not hold back from sharing how they wanted nothing to do with Rick and would refuse to listen to him if he ever shared anything during our processing sessions. Of course, they were not privy to the information Rick had shared with me the day before. I would have encouraged Rick to talk about it during group if he'd been there. I was clearly getting the feeling that the anger was still raw among the group members and perhaps it would be best if Rick took a break from group work for the time being. I was still on my mission to rehab Rick, and it was my full intention to reintroduce him to the group later on.

In the meantime, I had another challenge to deal with. My supervisor called me in for a meeting with Amy. Amy had informed my supervisor about her discomfort with the way the group was going and, in particular, her discomfort with Rick. The supervisor recommended I continue to lead the group on my own and Amy would be reassigned to another group with the less threatening geriatric patients. I proposed that it was important for the group to have some sort of closure first, but my supervisor said that now was not the right time. As Amy walked with me out of the meeting, she apologized for quitting the group. She disclosed to me that as a child she had been abused by an older family member, and Rick's similar behavior was opening old wounds. She did not go into detail, but she did say that when she'd told her family about the abuse, they were very dismissive and downplayed the incident that had hurt her so deeply years earlier.

I returned to my supervisor and conceded that Rick not resume group work until I felt he was ready. In the meantime, I wanted to prep the group for Rick's re-entry. They were not keen on the idea. Rick had missed only one week of group, but they felt they were already making better progress without the "perv" in the room. I told them that I would make sure that Rick would behave or else he would no longer be able to participate in group work. Our group had coalesced into a cohesive unit, and everyone agreed that we had a good thing going. I did not want to disrupt the cohesion, but I assured them that there were many other Ricks in the world, and it would be helpful for them to learn how to deal with people like him in an assertive and effective manner. After much cajoling and reassuring, I was able to convince them to allow Rick back in.

When Rick entered the next session, he was met with some angry stares. Some of the women just looked away. Amy was not there when we resumed the group sessions. This turned out to be serendipitous.

I was about to begin the group with a benign topic about stress management when Nicole stood up and pointed a finger at Rick. I was not sure whether she was going to attack him physically, so I moved my chair up to indicate that this session was not going to turn into a wrestling match. Nicole sternly said to Rick, "You owe Amy a big apology. We all saw how uncomfortable you made her feel, and I will not talk to you until you apologize to her in front of all of us." Rick looked around and saw the stares from the other women in the group, and he noticed the absence of Amy.

"She ain't here. So, what do you want me to do?"

I replied, "We can take care of that when Amy comes back."

Nicole, still standing in an aggressive posture, said, "Who says she *will* be back? Maybe she's terrified of Mr. Perv over here, and rightfully so. I have heard of psychos like Rick who stalk their therapist. She is probably gonna leave the hospital and never come back."

This was an opportunity to let the other voices in the room have a shot. Heather, who rarely spoke up in group, stood up and asked Rick to tell the group more about himself so that perhaps they could understand how he turned out this way. Heather was, in a sense, taking the place of Amy and acting as a co-therapist. This took everyone by surprise. You could feel the tension in the room as the group waited for Rick to speak up. Rick, who usually enjoyed being the center of attention, looked very uncomfortable. He leaned over and put his head in his hands. As he leaned over, his butt became somewhat exposed. Sha'day, another group member, took the opportunity to tell Rick that his butt was showing and said, "Not cool and very unattractive."

I sensed Rick becoming more tense and decided I needed to step in. "Rick, I know this is not the type of attention you like getting. But this is a group session and discomfort is something I addressed at the outset of our group. Maybe we can use some of that discomfort to help each other come to newfound insight."

Rick sighed and then began by talking about his upbringing with two parents who were both addicts. He talked of promises never fulfilled, porn collections, prostitution, and said matter-of-factly, "This is all I ever knew." After a brief pause, while everyone was mesmerized into silence by Rick's story, Rick got up and began pacing the room.

I could tell that this was becoming a breakthrough session and wanted to capitalize on it. Susan got up and walked over to Rick and put her hand on his shoulder. Rick seemed to melt at Susan's gesture. Susan was one of the senior members of the group. At age forty-five, she had been through her own challenges (which I did not know about fully at the time). She was a calming presence and was dealing with the loss of her son to an overdose. She looked Rick in the eyes and said, "Rick, my mother was also a prostitute and did God knows what. We are all here, as Jonathan says, to tell our stories." With that, Susan retreated to her seat. Rick returned to his seat and adjusted his shorts so they did not expose anything. Putting his head back in his hands, the group witnessed "Rick the Perv" transform into "Rick the innocent little boy" who had seen more than his share of misery. Rick started to sob. Between sobs, he said, "I'm sorry everybody. I feel bad for what I said."

Slowly, each group member approached Rick and patted him on the back. The session was truly transformative. The group members rightfully felt very proud of themselves and were no longer intimidated by Rick. Our now cohesive, dually diagnosed group decided that we needed a name for our little community. I suggested that they come up with ideas, write them on a slip of paper, and we would vote on the best name at our next group session.

That day Rick did not eat his lunch alone, or with me. He practiced proper etiquette while eating with other group members, who took notice of this change.

During our individual sessions, Rick and I continued to work through issues of pain, rejection, his need for attention, and general hygiene and etiquette. Rick was growing on me, as well as the other members of the group.

The question was how to bring Amy back into the group. This was trickier, although, in my opinion, absolutely necessary for the group to have some closure. Suffice it to say, Amy was traumatized by Rick. I explained to Amy that the group really wanted her to come back. I told her about how the group had discussed her absence and told her how we were about to give the group a name. After a bit more coaxing, Amy agreed to come back. As soon as Amy returned, she looked over at Rick.

I felt this session was going to be a deal-changer and was eager to see how this would all play out. Any anxiety that I would have had leading up to this moment was channeled into excitement that I might possibly complete my mission of rehabbing Rick. I felt as if the right words were being put in my mouth in just the right moments during that session.

Rick immediately got up and walked over to Amy and said, "Amy, I want to apologize for my behavior. I know I made you uncomfortable and for that I am very sorry. I want to apologize to you in front of our group and also apologize to the group for making everyone feel uncomfortable. You guys are like family to me and have accepted me even though I was disgusting to you." With that, Rick walked back to his seat. The group clapped, and Amy thanked Rick. Amy did not have to say much in response. I looked over to Amy and mouthed a "thank you" for stepping out of her comfort zone and returning.

The group members then came up with several clever names for the group and voted on the winning moniker: Out of the Cracks.

We ended the group by sharing our feelings about one another, with each group member saying at least three positive things about another group member. This positive experience reinforced things that had been stated earlier in our sessions. You can always find something admirable in the seemingly least admirable people. I also used this opportunity to inform the group that we would be closing the group down as my internship was ending the following week. The group, although disappointed, expressed their appreciation for learning to accept and care for everyone. They wanted to know what I would be doing. At the time, I had a job offer out of state, and I would likely be moving pending the successful completion of my dissertation requirements. I would also have to write up my experiences during the internship and give an oral presentation about something I gleaned from the internship experience. They unanimously encouraged me to share what happened in our group in my oral presentation.

I agreed to share this group experience with my graduate school class, along with the name they had chosen for themselves. I spoke about the evolution of the group and how Rick emerged from being a despised member of the group to a contributing one. My classmates all laughed after hearing about the chosen name. I hadn't thought the name had any relation to Rick's posterior, but my classmates suggested that this was probably why the group came up with the name! I was embarrassed about my naiveté. I'd thought the title was about the group's emergence from mental illness. The group had been truly transformative, after all. Perhaps the expression *double entendre* applies here.

I write this story more than twenty years after it happened. Over those years I have been amazed at the transformative nature of group work. Irv Yalom, the master group therapist, has truly been an inspiration to many, including me, and I have enjoyed every one of his books. Recently, Lori Gottlieb, another wonderful therapist and author of the bestseller *Maybe You Should Talk to Someone*, interviewed Irv Yalom about his life experiences. She mentioned that Irv has shared his humanity in the therapy room through his many books. Sometimes it is important to allow others into your life, especially in group work. Although it was difficult to relate to Rick at first, I felt I was able to connect with him just by saying that "I am a guy" and "I love basketball." Benign statements, but relatable. In Yalom's interview he mentioned something about "reuniting with the vital force" of sexual energy. I think this related to Rick. His inappropriate behavior with women and confusion about his own sexuality might have stemmed from the lack of nurturing from his mother. Together with all the issues with his father, it made more sense to me as well as the group members as to why Rick acted like a "perv" much of the time.

Rick's pivotal comment, "This is all I ever knew," struck a chord in every group member as they all realized that they too had perpetuated patterns learned from their families. Some group members were able to reflect on their own maladaptive patterns and many commented that if Rick could change, "we certainly can." Rick spent the last week of his outpatient stay having some one-on-one conversations with Susan. I would watch them from a distance and revel in Rick's ability to be more present. Susan, who was always easy to talk to, noticed me watching them in conversation. She later explained to me that she was not interested in a romantic relationship with Rick, but she was able to see Rick in a different way than before. I was grateful to Susan for her calming presence and her ability to see the good in everyone.

I have commented before that not all the people we treat are likable at first. Their unlikable behavior probably stems from the very mental illness they are being treated for. Many lack the awareness to understand how their behavior impacts others.

Oftentimes, relationships fail due to a lack of awareness of the impact of the conscious and subconscious messages we convey. If one spouse rolls their eyes when the other is trying to point out something important that is impacting their relationship, this could lead to a breakdown in communication. This can lead to what psychologist Martin Seligman coined as "learned help-lessness." They feel that they are not getting their message through to the intended recipient, so they decide it is hopeless to continue trying. This leads to conflict and resentment. Can you imagine how often this happens? That is why it takes a skilled therapist, coach, or manager to stop the action and point out where the breakdown seems to be occurring. This can happen in the context of group therapy as many members, aside from the therapists leading the group, begin to act as co-therapists by pointing out flaws and making suggestions on how to correct those flaws.

I genuinely believe that the group setting allows for these processes to evolve. Maybe we can all emerge from the proverbial "cracks" by allowing others to make honest and reflective comments on our behavior to optimize our human potential.

THE REDHEAD

The nature of life is change and the nature
of people is to resist change.
—Lori Gottlieb

The redhead stared and stared. What she was staring at
was never known. If you were to stand behind her and
follow the trajectory of her eyes, you would be more
baffled than ever. Staring, I have been told, makes people
smarter. Or, the colloquial "spacing out" makes you smarter. I'm
not sure about this, and it has not been scientifically proven. But
the redhead continued to stare. This was not a new behavior.

The redhead was originally referred to me by someone who
was loosely acquainted with me when I was an adjunct psychology professor. I agreed to take the case and was given minimal
information about this nineteen-year-old redhead named Rebecca.
The intake session certainly threw me off guard as Rebecca stood
for the first few minutes, refusing my offers for her to take a seat.
She would pace back and forth asking herself, "Why am I here?
Why am I here?" All of my efforts to engage her in conversation
failed. I tried to talk about things unrelated to therapy. I asked her
if she wanted to draw. I asked if she wanted to play a game. No
response. Finally, the pacing stopped, and she slumped down on

the couch. "There is no reason why I should be here," she repeated and plugged in her AirPods. I let her stay on the couch while she listened to whatever it was that she chose to listen to. She definitely was not in the mood to listen to a therapist. So I walked out to the waiting room where the young lady who drove her to the appointment was sitting. I explained to her that it was evident that Rebecca did not want to be here, and it might be best if she drove her back home.

However, her driver, who was her roommate, Hannah, insisted that I try to do something. She had grown increasingly nervous over the past few weeks the longer Rebecca would go into staring mode. It was because of Hannah's urging that Rebecca started therapy. I was wondering whether Rebecca had had some sort of psychotic break. In fact, I questioned whether Rebecca was even her real name. She often didn't respond to that name when I would say it, nor when Hannah would say it. I began referring to her as the redhead.

I am a therapist. I chose this profession because I was told that I was good at working with people, especially those who presented with mysterious psychopathology. I was turned on to the field after reading books by Oliver Sacks who, as a neurologist, pondered many baffling mysteries of the brain and worked with many individuals with rather interesting manifestations of neuropathology. I began reading other books by Dr. Sacks, but the first one I read was *The Man Who Mistook His Wife for a Hat*.

It is always interesting to reflect back as to how someone begins therapy and who that person chooses to see as their therapist. I was not Rebecca's first therapist. In fact, she could not remember what number therapist I was. One thing was for sure: I was her first male therapist. I did not readily accept her as a client. I generally avoid seeing young adult females with severe pathology. From past experience, I had to deal with this population who would test boundaries and misinterpret the nature of a therapeutic relationship. I had been burnt before and did not want to enter that arena again.

I agreed to see Rebecca with a couple of stipulations. Sessions had to end after fifty minutes promptly. No sessions would be held at night, and there had to be someone else in the office suite while we were in session. Rebecca signed the document—staring at me—without saying a word. *Did she understand what she was signing?* I wondered. To make certain, I asked her to read the entire document, look me in the eye, and say that she understood. At that point, she got up and left the office in a huff. I sat there dumbfounded. I had never seen this before. Honestly, I was relieved that she had left. However, the relief did not last long enough.

Five minutes later, she was back, knocking on my door. She gently opened the door and stood there, once again staring at me. I was considering asking her to leave or I would be calling the police when suddenly she looked down and slid onto the couch. Slowly looking up, she apologized for her earlier behavior and said she was nervous about coming to therapy. In my own mind, all sorts of red flags went off. I am certainly not a fan of dramatics. The staring was definitely off-putting. Her defiance of my rules certainly did not make me comfortable. Her past history with other therapists was reason enough for me to throw in the proverbial therapeutic towel before we got in too deep. She seemed better suited for an inpatient setting. I tried addressing her by her name but got no reaction. I was tempted to call her "Red" to shock her out of her trance but thought better of it. So, I did what I do best. I remained silent and stared back. Her discomfort mounting, she put a stop to the silence and finally started talking. "Sorry. If I am here, I might as well use the time."

Her persona radically changed once she started talking. She possessed an elegant voice with a slight British accent, although it seemed like she was just putting on the accent. She apologized at least twice more during the session. She talked about her history, which seemed both sad and impressive at the same time. She was born out of wedlock to an alcoholic mother. Her father was apparently a fellow addict she had met at a meeting. Their one night together had produced my client. Her mother had been absent from her life until she was two years old. During that time, she was cared for by her grandmother and her grandmother's boyfriend. Her mother apparently had taken the time to clean herself up and maintain steady employment for the six months prior to taking Rebecca back. Another impetus for her taking Rebecca was that her mother's boyfriend had been seen fondling Rebecca on multiple occasions. Grandma threw him out with the dishwater. Rebecca's mother enrolled in college, where she excelled and obtained a degree in political science. She then went to law school and finished among the top of her class. According to Rebecca, her mother currently works for a top law firm as a litigator specializing in domestic disputes and child abuse cases. She also volunteers at a shelter for runaway girls. Rebecca articulated this historical information with passion and pride that her mother was able to get her act together and ended her soliloquy with, "I just wish that I too could get my act together."

I continued to press on for more information as to why she was coming in for therapy. At first, she looked at me and said, "Why not?" but quickly apologized again. "I am sorry that I am acting like this, but my respect for therapy and therapists has diminished over time." Almost anticipating my next question, Rebecca stated, "I know what you are thinking. I will tell you why I am here. I really need help. I think I hurt someone." Seeing my vacant expression, she explained, "Actually, I know I have hurt someone. I know I have hurt many people, but I don't know how to stop. And no, I don't mean physically, so you don't have to report me...yet." At that point, she smiled and seemed to loosen up a bit.

"Rebecca," I started, "I am glad that you had the courage to come in to meet with me, but I am not sure I can help you." I let those words sit for a while. Rebecca looked down and played with her purse strings. I continued the silence and decided that it would not be I who would break it. Unfortunately, it was Rebecca's cell phone that broke the silence. The next apology came as she put her phone on silent. "I am so sorry for that. I usually turn it off when something important..." she stopped herself before completing her sentence. She looked at her watch and asked, "Is our time up?" I was tempted to allow her to continue her story out of sheer curiosity but stuck to my fifty-minute rule.

"Yes. Our session is over, but I want you to consider how you want to proceed and what your true expectations are for therapy. Therapy is very personal and private. I know Hannah is very involved in your life and cares deeply about your psychological welfare, but this is *your* therapy, and I am *your* therapist who will individualize your therapy to suit your needs."

Rebecca thanked me and walked out, looking back once to see what my reaction was. I was standing up and holding my notepad. I know I had a bit of concern on my face and hoped she wouldn't notice.

I consciously put this session out of my mind because I did not treasure the idea of becoming roped into Rebecca's drama. However, I did make a mental note to make Rebecca the main topic of my next session with my supervisor, Dr. Charlie Wang. Charlie and I had developed a wonderful collegial relationship over the years, though he was superior to me in age and experience with the borderline client. I believed that Rebecca would classify as borderline according to any expert in psychopathology. Borderline clients are mostly females with very poor boundaries and poor impulse control. They also tend to talk about suicide and make threats of suicide when they don't get what they want.

Dr. Charlie Wang had quite an interesting life of his own. When we first met, he made it clear that he was an atheist and that he was gay. As was my typical operational style, I maintained my poker face. He then went on to explain he felt the need to share this information at our first meeting because he wanted to be very careful not to blur the lines of religiosity and psychotherapy. I stared into his eyes and said one word: "Baloney." He gave me a nervous-sounding chuckle, realizing that that explanation was one that I had probably heard a dozen times, whenever someone felt the need to share their sexual orientation—unsolicited. He then continued, "I see that you are a religious man (nodding at my yarmulke), and I wanted to make sure you were comfortable having me supervise you." I continued with the poker face. "Okay...", he said, "I admit that I thought that you might be judging me and would always feel like you had to be on guard, so I wanted to put that out before we began the supervisory relationship."

I replied, "Thank you for your honesty."

From that point on, Charlie and I maintained a wonderful relationship, and we laughed at our culture's stereotypes. We would frequently meet at his favorite coffee shop. A coffee drinker myself, I understood what he meant when he said he was able to "think" better after a good "cup of Joe." We would find a quiet corner to sit and discuss cases, frequently making up funny pseudonyms for the clients we discussed.

I digress for a moment by sharing this information about my supervisor and our relationship. I have been in many supervisory relationships—sometimes on the receiving end of the supervision and sometimes providing the supervision. I have had supervisors who were amazing and helpful and others who were quite unprofessional or simply not good in their role.

I believe every therapist should have a supervisor or, at the very least, a fellow colleague with whom they can bounce ideas around. The supervisory relationship is based on trust. One supervisor had broken my trust by sharing personal information that I had shared during supervision. Another supervisor was so rigid that he told me how unprofessional it was to meet at coffee shops. So, I had become cautious until meeting Charlie.

Dr. Charlie Wang had a different style. He was laid back and possessed a great sense of humor. He had been married before to a woman before coming out as gay. He and his now ex-wife continue to have a very amicable relationship, which I find commendable. At our caffeinated supervisory sessions, he was not a stickler for suggested guidelines and would frequently express his frustration at the current climate of the psychological community. He railed against the psychology boards for being too stiff, and he thought psychology boards were composed of people who generally lacked common sense. He is a huge fan of Irvin Yalom, as I am, and we frequently discuss Yalom's works during our sessions. In *The Gift of Therapy*, Yalom wrote about the unfortunate climate where psychologists are forced to refrain from doing things that resemble acting like a human.

I have also found Charlie to be a very compassionate man who would at times become very emotional when discussing his upbringing. He admitted that he has cried with clients as they shared their stories and stated that it would be counterintuitive to *not* mirror the emotions of clients who were emotionally pained and needed their therapist to "match emotions" as he liked to put it. I have taken the idea of matching emotions, especially after working with a client who said he did not like working with happy therapists. (See the chapter "I Don't Like Happy Therapists" in my first book *The Guilt Trap and Other Tales of Psychotherapy*.)

I greatly looked forward to discussing the "redhead" with Charlie at our next meeting. He greeted me with his usual fist bump as we sat down at Starbucks. He ordered his frap, while I stuck to my plain old coffee. Over the years, Charlie grew accustomed to reading my facial expressions. He immediately said, "So you have a new client, and you are unsure how to proceed."

"I am unsure *whether* to proceed. That is the question," I countered.

Charlie stared me down as we have both done when we felt we needed a moment of contemplation. It is interesting how comfortable I am with pregnant pauses and awkward silence. I find them powerful. (My family members, on the other hand, can't stand my silent moments.)

Charlie broke the silence: "Jonathan, I know you very well. I will hear you out. I get this feeling that you don't want to continue with whatever you are dealing with, but it is probably essential for you to continue based on past experiences I have had with you and your most difficult clients. Trust me. I've got your back and will make sure you don't get too overwhelmed."

I knew Charlie was right, but I wanted to present him with the transference that occurred during my initial session with Rebecca. We spoke about Rebecca's vacant stares and her decision to return to therapy, and with me in particular. I brought up every conceivable red flag. Charlie did not seem fazed. Instead, he said with his compassionate tone, "Jonathan, you have been burned before. It's perfectly logical for you to feel ambivalent about Rebecca's case. However, Rebecca came to you for help. Her reasons for choosing you are irrelevant for now. If they become relevant and concerning as you progress, we can readdress it."

It was clear that I was letting my own countertransference get in the way. I was afraid that I would end up investing too much mental energy in this case. But for the time being, Rebecca needed my help. After my second cup of coffee and some sage tips from Charlie, I decided to walk home. During my walk, I thought about therapy in general and Rebecca in particular. Therapy had been my calling for so long. Over the many years of practicing, I have been blessed with learning from and helping numerous clients. I have also learned that therapy comes with pitfalls unlike any other profession I can think of. I exposed my own challenges in my first book, *The Guilt Trap and Other Tales of Psychotherapy.* I used to refer to them as failings, but I now have rephrased that term to challenges and opportunities for growth. No therapist is flawless. We all slip up along the way. Having a supervisor like Charlie has certainly helped me curtail some of those slip-ups and has offered me a more positive perspective on the work I do. Charlie often points out that I am becoming too rigid, which I find to be one of the biggest insults in my profession. Charlie was using reverse psychology on his supervisee. I still love his style—and brutal honesty.

The next day, Rebecca left a message that she wanted to have a double session. I instinctively wrote back that this would not be possible even though technically I could have made it possible. I had informed her during the first session that I do not accept text messages except for scheduling or canceling sessions. Before hitting the send button, I quickly phoned Charlie. He did not respond, so I went with my instinct and hit "Send." I was happy that I sent it because Rebecca immediately responded that she wanted to hold off the next session. I put Rebecca out of my mind for a couple of days and immersed myself in my Talmudic studies. Studying the Talmud transports me to a new dimension. When I focus solely on the give and take from the ancient Talmudic scholars, it invigorates me.

The next morning, I received a phone call from what was listed as a private number, I hesitated for a moment and then answered. The call was from Hannah, Rebecca's friend. Hannah told me that she was concerned about Rebecca because of a post she'd left on her Facebook account. The post was cryptic. She read it to me before I had a chance to say anything: "Not sure how I'm gonna continue. Sorry to all those I hurt."

I thanked Hannah for reaching out to me, but informed her that I did not have consent to speak with her. She said, "I understand, but I thought, as her therapist, you should know." I thanked her again and hung up the phone.

In the meantime, Charlie called me back. I filled him in about Rebecca's request for a double session, my demurral, and the subsequent call from Hannah with her concern about Rebecca. Charlie suggested that I call back and offer her the double session. "During the session, I would try to ask her about friends that she uses as a 'lifeline,'" he suggested. "While discussing that, Jonathan, you should perhaps ask her to allow you to speak with Hannah." I was thinking along the same lines, but it was comforting to hear the advice being echoed by Charlie.

I called Rebecca back with the intention of informing her that I could get her in for a double session the next morning. She did not answer. I waited but had difficulty concentrating on anything else for the rest of that day. I waited and waited for her to return my call, but by eleven o'clock that night I had no response. In previous years, I probably would have tried again to call a client I believed was in crisis. But this time I decided to sleep on it and not try too hard to reach her.

That night, sleep did not come easy. After tossing and turning, I finally fell asleep but awoke from a terrible dream. In the dream, I saw a woman who looked to be in her forties standing on a bridge and staring down at her reflection. The woman looked nothing like Rebecca aside for one feature. She had red hair. The woman was looking up at the sky and shaking her head violently. Then something fell out of her pants pocket. It was a cell phone. The woman tried to retrieve it before it fell into the murky brown water below. The dream ended with the woman reaching down into the water with an extended hand.

At that point, I woke up shaking. Not wanting to wake up my wife, I walked into my home office with my phone to check my messages. There were three messages. One was from a telemarketer promising me that I would make $10,000 if I listened to the following IMPORTANT announcement. The next one was from Charlie, saying that he would be available in the morning to talk, and the third message was from Hannah. I listened carefully to the message. She said, "Hi, Dr. Lasson. I know you can't speak with me. I did hear back from Rebecca. She sounded weird. As if she was on something. I know she doesn't use drugs and rarely drinks, but her words were slurred. She called to say not to worry about her and that she was at home watching a movie on Netflix. Just wanted to let you know. Bye."

I was somewhat relieved to hear that Rebecca was home. I checked the time of Hannah's call. It was 2:36 a.m. That gave me even more comfort as I realized that Rebecca was probably in her bed, falling asleep to a movie. Her slurred speech, though, was concerning. I tried to go back to sleep, but it didn't work. So I opened my prayer book and said some of my morning prayers. I prayed for Rebecca, and I prayed to G-d to give me the wisdom and strength to be able to help Rebecca. I then went back to my office to catch up on some notes I had to write for another client, Andy, who I was seeing for his anxiety about animals. Andy was a ten-year-old who was petrified of dogs and cats. His parents were terrific parents, and Andy was a motivated boy who knew his fears were irrational but needed some help getting over them. I reflected on how Andy compared with Rebecca. Realizing that there was no comparison, I found myself thinking how G-d sends me some "easy" clients to balance out the more difficult ones. After finishing my notes on Andy, I looked up to a beautiful prayer that hangs in my office called the "Doctor's Prayer." This is a Hebrew prayer that many doctors say before they start their day working with patients and clients with medical and mental issues. I read the prayer and reflected on the words, "Please grant me the merit to help those who seek me out." Rebecca had sought me out. I did not have the right to make excuses to avoid helping her.

I went outside and took a short walk around the block. It was a beautiful, sunny day and no one in my family was awake. I came home and checked on my then-five-year-old daughter, who the night before had not been feeling well. She was sound asleep. At eight-thirty, my phone rang. It was our family pediatrician's office calling to let us know that our daughter had tested positive for strep. I sent a WhatsApp message to my wife to let her know, and then I drove to my other office, where I had begun seeing clients. In the past, I had used my basement office to see some clients but had decided to move all clients to my other office that I subleased from another psychologist. This arrangement made life much less complicated, as my home office was not as private as I had wanted. I did not have any clients until ten that morning, so I sat down on my office couch and closed my eyes.

My cell phone woke me up at about nine-thirty. On the one hand, I was hoping it was Rebecca, and on the other hand, I was happy to see that it was my neurologist's office trying to schedule another appointment. For years, I had suffered from terrible headaches until this neurologist told me I was suffering from vestibular migraines. The medicine had been working and thankfully the headaches were becoming manageable. Shortly after I hung up, the phone rang again. This time it indeed was Rebecca.

I could hear Rebecca, but I also heard a man's voice in the background. Rebecca sounded completely lucid and told me that she wanted to meet for another appointment. There was no slur in her voice, and her slight British accent that I'd picked up on during our first session was not noticeable. It was kind of strange. I heard Rebecca scream out, "Shut up! I'm on an important call with my therapist." So much for keeping her sessions confidential. The man in the background shouted some expletive, and then a door slammed.

I asked Rebecca if everything was okay and she said, "Yeah, just the usual drama." I scheduled for her to come in the next morning at nine o'clock. After the phone call, I thought that things didn't really add up. I thought she had been watching Netflix by herself the night before. I made a note to try to address it during our next session.

The next day I was up super early, made myself some coffee, and after a brisk walk headed over to my office. While catching up on emails and notes, Rebecca walked into the waiting room. Although Rebecca was early for her appointment, I decided to stop what I was doing and bring her in earlier than scheduled.

Rebecca was dressed more like a college student than a professional. As I escorted her into the room, there was a noticeable scent of alcohol emanating from her. Rebecca slumped down on the couch and crossed her arms, staring out the window. Her red hair was tied with a black ponytail holder. I started the session by asking why she came so early. She shrugged her shoulders, still staring out the window. I reminded myself of my prayer to help her as best as I could, and I figured the best way to help her was to not say anything at all. After a few minutes, Rebecca diverted her gaze from the window and reached into her pants pocket to retrieve her cell. Finally, she looked up at me and asked, "What should I do first?"

Without pause, I said, "First, you should turn off your cell phone. Don't put it on vibrate. Just turn it off. Right now, you need to stay focused while I say some things to you. In order for this to work, I need your full attention. Staring out the window and looking at your cell phone every now and then will not benefit you in therapy. I also need for you to be very honest with me. You will get much more from our sessions if we are honest with each other. Do you understand me?" Rebecca nodded. "Rebecca," I continued,

"I don't consider a nod as acknowledgment to an agreement. I need you to use your words, so I am clear that we have an understanding here. Otherwise, I will need to suggest that you see someone else who is willing to work with you the way you want."

I chose these words very carefully, making sure she knew that she was ultimately in charge of the therapy outcome. At this point, I was not sure how Rebecca would respond. I was expecting the worst but instead got an "I am so sorry, Dr. Lasson. I am so sorry." Then the tears came. I sat there and watched her cry for what seemed like an hour. I offered her tissues, which she accepted, and asked, "Rebecca, where are all these tears coming from?" Rebecca, in between sobs, stated, "I think I am hurting people." Using my "I need" tactic, I continued, "Rebecca, you said that during our first session, and I am really confused by what you mean by 'hurt someone.' I need you to explain what you mean when you say that. I also want to ask about who was with you in your apartment while I was on the phone with you."

Once Rebecca regained her composure, she said, "Dr. Lasson, I don't intentionally hurt people. I've had some really bad relationships in my life, and I know I am at fault for some of them. I lead boyfriends on, and then I say something really mean to them. Just like the guy I had over when I was on the phone with you. Last year, one of my boyfriends committed suicide and left a note. His mom would not let me read it, but I could tell from her expression that she thought I was to blame."

Rebecca then went on to share about four or five other relationships that ended poorly. Rebecca had a pattern. When she was feeling low, she would dress up and go to a bar and bring home someone she had flirted with. After being with that "boyfriend," she would show her true colors, become enraged by something, and throw them out. There was a pattern, and I needed to find a way to break it. I asked her about how she'd met the most recent guy. "A repeat customer," was Rebecca's reply. Seeing my vacant expression, Rebecca explained that she had first met him the same way she met many other guys. He had called her back for some reason months after she'd thrown him out and wanted to go out again. Rebecca had not changed and treated him as poorly as the first time they had met.

I asked Rebecca for some clarification as to why she felt she had hurt these people if they chose to be with her. She went on to explain her history of being a mean, condescending girl who would only associate with popular people. She felt that her history of abuse contributed to this need to feel some sort of love, as superficial as it may be, she still felt it was love—for the moment. Once she realized that she had no concept of love, she lost respect for her body and used it as a method of attaining a temporary fix.

Rebecca had clarified what I had been thinking but was not able to put into proper words. Rebecca did not necessarily have an addiction. I did not think she would be a good candidate for group therapy. Rather, Rebecca had a strong need to belong. Before ending the session, I commended Rebecca on being honest with me and reassured her that her honesty would help her along in the process.

I called Charlie to schedule a "cup of Joe supervision session." When I met with Charlie, we discussed Rebecca and what emerged during our sessions. He asked me if I was still giving any consideration to the borderline diagnosis. I told Charlie that I was ambivalent about assigning her that label.

Charlie then made a great observation. He said that he had noticed that I was burnt before by previous clients with this diagnosis and that my ambivalence about putting Rebecca in that category may be my effort to keep her going as long as possible. "Remember how you were very strict with your rules for agreeing to therapy with her?" I nodded. "Perhaps your strict adherence to these rules has paid off in some way." I let Charlie continue his train of thought, liking what I was hearing. "Jonathan, the people that you work with are not always the most likable people in the world. In the past, you were an out-of-the-box thinker and clinician, and I think you still are, with some of the more cut-and-dry clients you work with. Let's assume that Rebecca has been playing you this whole time and giving you information that would only endear her to you. What would you have done in the past and what would you do now?"

This is one of the reasons why I cherish my supervision from Charlie. I love how real he is whenever we meet. Whenever he does this to me, I sort of melt and tell all.

Feeling totally vulnerable (in a good way), I said, "I would have given my all for the client, put up barriers after it was already too late, and obsessed about what I could have done differently. And as to your next question about what I have learned from my past handling of people like Rebecca, I have learned not to overcompensate and turn into a rock."

Charlie smiled, knowing I had anticipated his question and appreciated his wisdom and style. Patting me on the back, he smiled and said, "Precisely!"

I looked down at my cup of coffee and pondered what was going on. Charlie allowed me to have this quiet time. I thought I was the expert at pregnant pauses. But Charlie took it to a new level. After seeing that he had given me enough time, he smiled again and asked, "So, how is your coffee?"

"It is fluid and liquid," I responded, letting him know I understood his advice was to go with the flow. Charlie laughed, and I smiled, feeling so appreciative for having someone to bounce around ideas.

Charlie suggested that I have Rebecca keep a journal that she writes in immediately after each session. I should ask her to document immediate reflections from the session, takeaways from the sessions that will help her, and questions that she would like to bring to the next session.

Rebecca came on time to the next session. She said that she was really ready to do some hard work. I asked her what that would look like for her. She said that she would have to look at her past relationship failures and learn how to break the patterns. She then admitted that she was not always present during the sessions. She admitted that at times she was thinking about the night before. This was the ideal time to bring up the suggestion for journaling. Keeping to Charlie's script, I pressed her to write down immediate thoughts. We practiced this first in session by playing a free association game. I would say a word and she would have to say the first thing that came to mind. I told her not to censor herself. She should go with her first thought. She seemed to enjoy the game and giggled at some of her responses. She asked me if I was writing everything down. I assured her that I was and reminded her that all her responses were confidential. After about ten minutes, I asked her what she felt about this free association game. She thought for a little and said, "I guess it is helping me be more present during the session. As I told you earlier, I sometimes just drift off."

This last comment got me thinking, and I shared an observation of my own. "Rebecca, when I first met you, I noticed that you would just stare off at seemingly nothing. Can you share a little about what goes through your mind when you do that?"

Rebecca went on to explain that she had always been kind of spacey as a kid. Her teachers recommended that she see the school counselor. She did not like the school counselor because she was old and made assumptions about her. She would constantly ask her if she was being abused and even went so far as to say, "I know you are being abused, so let's talk about that." Rebecca said that although the counselor was right, and she was being abused by her mother's boyfriend, she did not feel it was her business to ask her and that she was not ready to disclose it to "this woman at that time." The counselor reported her suspicions to the principal who contacted Rebecca's mother. A meeting was scheduled at the school. The principal, the school counselor, and the mother were all there and Rebecca sat quietly, staring off into space. When the counselor said straight out what she thought was happening, Rebecca denied it. Her mother also said she had no reason to believe it and began screaming at the counselor and berating her for putting her daughter through such trauma. Rebecca's mother grabbed her by the arm and marched her out of the office. She kept Rebecca home the rest of the year and then enrolled her at a different school.

Once enrolled in her new school, Rebecca became "Miss Popular." No one questioned her about what was going on at home and the boyfriend was out of the house anyway. Rebecca excelled in some areas academically but would toe the line when it came to rules of the school. She would not wear her school uniform according to the school's policies and would be disrespectful to her teachers, at times. She was doing generally well in terms of her social life and had made many new friends. She would host parties at her house and her mother was more than happy to supply her with food and movies for her friends when they had sleepovers. Rebecca said she felt her mother was less worried when friends were at her house as opposed to Rebecca sleeping out.

Rebecca remained popular although she would alienate some of the less popular kids. The principal spoke to her about being kinder, but she continued on in her ways, even shoving a girl who called her a snob. This landed her a suspension and a grounding from her mother.

As she got to the end of middle school, Rebecca began acting out more. She discovered that the boys were paying more attention to her, and she developed a reputation that did not earn her any honors from the adults, but her popularity continued among her peers as she became student body president. Rebecca was known for her acting and dancing abilities and the star of many school productions.

Rebecca never regarded her self-destructive relationships as destructive. She just thought she was having fun and that she was always in control. Indeed, many of the boys she would break up with would come back to her for the wrong reasons.

We discussed the effects of the abuse she endured when she was younger. She minimized it by saying flippantly, "Dr. Lasson, doesn't that happen to everybody?" I corrected her with the most current stats on sexual abuse in children and explained that different kids have different outcomes.

"Does that make me more resilient?" she asked, "Because I really don't think it made too much of a difference in my life?"

"Perhaps," I responded, "but I am more curious how you developed a reputation as someone who goes through relationships the same way some people flip channels until they find the right show. Then they get sick of that show and move on to a new one."

She thought about my flipping channels analogy for a while and said, "Maybe I just get bored with things quicker than others."

"Rebecca, you are obviously a bright and articulate woman. I would think you would be able to find more meaning in your relationships than being a shallow channel flipper." I was going out on a limb with that assumption of intellect, but something struck me about her, and I assumed that she was probably more capable than her grades in school suggested. Plus, I had a backup argument in case she challenged me...which she did.

"What makes you think I am so smart?" she challenged. "You never gave me an IQ test."

"I am so glad you mentioned that, Rebecca. I am willing to bet that you have at least above average intelligence. You had mentioned that you did well in classes that you liked but only applied yourself when you wanted to. I would like to have you tested, as long as you promise to give it your all. Another thing, look at your mother. She ended up going to law school and really applying herself after all she went through. You admired her determination. What makes you think you couldn't do the same?"

This argument seemed to really get to Rebecca. I could feel that she was becoming more present and that for this game of intellect she was very present. She then asked me what an IQ test entailed and why she couldn't just take one online. I explained to her the components of the test and that online tests have zero validity and reliability.

"I remember those terms from my stats class," Rebecca responded. "I did okay in that class. We had a pretty good teacher. As for my mother, I am not sure I am as strong as she is."

I decided a compliment was in order. "Rebecca, I must say I am impressed with you."

"Why? We're just talking. I am not committing to anything. At least not yet."

"I am impressed with how present you are today during this session. I feel that you are here, and you are with me in conversation."

Rebecca did not know what to do with this, which I kind of expected. She remained quiet, absorbed in thought.

"You're not saying much, Rebecca."

"I don't usually hear compliments about how smart I am. Usually the compliments are about my looks."

"So how does it feel to be complimented on something other than looks?"

"Weird…and fake," was her response.

"Do you think I was complimenting you to flatter you?" I asked.

"I don't know. Were you?"

"No. I was sincere. But I am assuming this is not something you are used to, and I want to train you about how to receive a compliment."

"How are you going to do that?"

"I want you to give me a compliment. It can be fake if you want."

Rebecca thought for a second and smiled. "Okay, I've got one. Dr. Lasson, you are a great therapist."

I responded, "Thank you, Rebecca. I really appreciate that."

"I am not good at *giving* compliments either," she responded.

"Well, that was a pretty nice one," I replied.

"Well, it was fake. JK. I think I meant it."

"So, let's break down how I received your compliment. What did I say?"

"You said, 'Thank you.'"

"That's not all I said."

"What else did you say? Oh. You said my name."

"Good. Was there anything else I said?"

"Not that I can remember."

"Okay. There was something else that I said that is very important when receiving compliments. But before I tell you, why was it important that I said your name?"

She hesitated for a bit and looked directly at me. "It actually felt good that you said my name. I'm not sure why."

"Rebecca," I repeated, and she giggled. "Do people call you other names besides Rebecca?"

"I get called lots of nasty names, but Mom calls me Becca. Hannah calls me Becky."

"What does it say on your birth certificate?" I asked.

"Rebecca McKenzie," she replied.

"That's a nice name. There is something else I said when you complimented me on being a good therapist. I said, 'I appreciate it.' What does that do for someone when those three words are added?"

"I guess it gives more value."

"Why is that?"

"I guess when you appreciate something," she responded after thinking about it, "it gives more value to whatever it is that you are saying."

"Brilliant," I responded with a British accent.

Rebecca started laughing.

"What is so funny?" I continued with the fake accent.

"Your fake accent. You need to work on that, so don't quit your day job."

"Well, you put on the same accent sometimes. I meant to ask you about that."

"Yeah, I do that sometimes. Not sure why. I did act a lot in school, so maybe it just stuck with me. I think the British sound smarter, I guess."

We sat there processing our discussion. Rebecca still seemed present.

Striking while the iron was still hot, I decided to talk about the idea of testing and journaling.

"Rebecca, I want you to start a project for you and me. After each session, I want you to write down your takeaways from each session and write down any questions you want to bring to the next session. At some point, I would also like to refer you for cognitive testing."

"Okay. I can do that. Maybe we can put the testing on hold, though. Is our time up?"

Looking at my clock, I realized we had gone over by a few minutes. "Yes. Our time is up."

Rebecca remained sitting on the couch and let out a yawn.

"Tired?" I asked.

"Yeah. Not sure why, though. I stopped at Starbucks before I came today."

"Being present is something you are not used to and that can be draining. Today you were present almost the entire time. I am proud of you."

Rebecca blushed and stood up. Turning toward the door, she slowly walked and then stopped in her tracks. Turning back to me, she smiled and said, "Thank you, Dr. Lasson. I really appreciate that."

I gave her the thumbs up for successfully receiving a compliment, and she walked out with more of a spring in her step.

As she left, I felt proud of how I had handled the situation. I smiled for Rebecca.

The therapeutic relationship comes with its ups and downs. When things are moving in the right direction, I like to go with the momentum.

I called Charlie and left him a message that I just wanted to run something by him. Charlie called back within ten minutes. I told him about today's session and how good it felt that Rebecca was actually present and attentive. I then asked him if I should contact her the next day just to remind her about the journaling or if that would be too much.

I was not expecting the answer Charlie gave. "Too much! Jonathan. Have you lost your mind? She has chosen you to help her. If you took the time to call me to ask me that question, what do you think my answer is going to be?"

"Gosh, Charlie," I said somewhat cynically, "have you had coffee yet today?"

"Jonathan, you are either becoming overly rigid and overcompensating for being too caring of a therapist or you have simply gone crazy. You still pray for your clients, correct?"

"Yes," I responded, a little taken aback. I knew Charlie was not praying for his clients as he did not believe in that, but he did take a "whatever works" approach similar to mine.

"So you can call her and give her a reminder as well. She does not have a great track record of following through, so I would say you would be irresponsible if you did not call to give her a reminder."

I thought for a second and then said, "Thanks, Charlie. I really appreciate your advice." Now I was officially practicing what I was preaching.

I realized at that point that Charlie was so right. I was overcompensating. My previous supervisor was so rigid that I would never have gotten away with such a phone call. Her rigidity was messing with my persona of a "whatever works therapist." I would still maintain my boundaries that I had initially set up, but Charlie was right. I had to loosen up.

Rebecca came in, and for the next few sessions, surprised herself—and her therapist. She was attentive and followed through with the suggestions I gave. She journaled on a regular basis and was really enjoying the writing piece. She even said that she would like to write a memoir someday. (I guess I did not have to remind her about journaling.) She was also more noticeably present. The vacant staring seemed to be a thing of the past.

At some point, I asked Rebecca if she thought it would be a good idea to bring Hannah in for a session. She thought for a moment and said, "I'm not sure what good that would do. Do you think it is necessary?"

"Sometimes it is good to hear from someone who knows you really well how they experience the changes they see. Hannah has always been there for you and was the one who encouraged you to seek help in the first place," I responded.

"Let me think about that one and get back to you." After a pause, she continued, "Dr. Lasson, I want to ask you something which has been on my mind since we began therapy."

I had an inkling what she might ask but was certainly curious.

"I mentioned to you that I never knew my father. I also told you about my mother's abusive boyfriend. We kind of discussed the possibility of how my hurting other people, especially men, had to do with my past. I think there is something to that, but I was wondering something. If I met my actual father, do you think it would do anything positive for me?"

"I am not sure, Rebecca. What would you hope it would do for you?"

"I honestly don't know, but I do wonder what the man that helped bring me into this world was like. I would be prepared for disappointment though because that has been my pattern until recently. I know I am moving in the right direction, though."

"What type of disappointment are you preparing for?"

"Well...he could be dead for all I know," Rebecca said while suppressing a laugh. "Then I'll never know what he was like."

"What else?"

"Maybe my mom doesn't even know who he is or how to reach him. Maybe she wouldn't want me knowing who he is."

"What about the boyfriend? Would you want some sort of closure there as well?"

"I don't think so. I don't really care about him, and I don't think about him as much as I think about my biological father."

"Okay. I think I can understand that. So, do you want to speak with your mother about your biological father?"

"I already asked to meet with her, but I did not tell her why. She agreed to meet this Friday."

"Are you nervous?"

"A little. I've never really spoken to her much about this. I imagine she wants to put it behind her. Probably embarrassing for her. But then I was thinking that she probably would not want me to follow the same path she had, so maybe she would be okay with it."

We were both silent for a little while. Again, I was impressed with Rebecca's ability to remain present, and I wanted to address it. I used the silence to let things sit.

"Dr. Lasson, do you know what I am thinking about now?"

"I can guess. Would you like me to do that?"

"Yes!"

"I believe you are charting new territory. You feel more confident, and your answers are reflective of my direct questions. You also are using our therapeutic silences effectively."

"Well…that is mostly accurate. I wasn't aware of the therapeutic silences. But yes…I have been feeling more confident lately. That is what I was thinking about. Can you tell me more about this therapeutic silence stuff?"

"Sure. Therapeutic silence is exactly as it sounds. It is not the same as staring, though. By not exchanging any words, you have time to reflect on what was just said and let it sink in. Sometimes the discomfort caused by the silence forces us to confront our true feelings."

"Who is supposed to break that silence?"

"There are no rules for who initiates the break. I usually am the one waiting for the other person to break the silence in most cases."

"I kind of like the silence. Not sure why. Maybe it's just new to me and I am enjoying having quiet time. I never considered my staring off as silent because so many voices were swirling around my head at the same time. That was noisy!"

"I take it that your life has been pretty hectic?"

"I think I choose to make it that way. Correction. I chose to make it that way. Past tense," Rebecca smiled proudly. "I was also thinking more about Hannah. I would like for her to come in and have a joint session. I want to know what she actually is seeing in me and our relationship."

"Okay. Let's set that up whenever it is convenient for the two of you. I can also hear you out about meeting with your mother and what you would like to accomplish."

"Sounds good."

As Rebecca left the office that day, I thought about people hitting low points and then emerging as resilient human beings. I am always impressed when people find that inner strength to help propel them to greater levels of functioning. Rebecca was doing just that. My concerns at the start of therapy were no longer a big deal. The red flags had turned green. I was curious about the transformation and was excited about our session with Hannah. Another perspective would certainly be useful.

Rebecca confirmed that Hannah would indeed be attending the next session. As is the case most of the time, our impressions of who someone is and what they actually look like don't always match. Hannah was certainly not the person I imagined. I had imagined someone similar to Rebecca, with a well-put-together style. But dressed in workout clothing, Hannah was small and plain. Hannah apologized for her attire, and Rebecca quickly interjected, "Don't worry, Dr. Lasson is not judging you." Hannah then sat beside Rebecca on the couch and made herself comfortable by rearranging the pillows.

Rebecca did not seem to have prepped Hannah as to why she was at today's appointment. So I began by telling Hannah that Rebecca and I felt it would be useful to have her come in and give a perspective from someone who lived with her.

Hannah looked around the office and admired the simplicity of the décor. She mentioned that she sees a therapist regularly and that she often gets distracted by all the gadgets in her therapist's office. She seemed very comfortable in her own skin and quickly shifted back to the reason why she was there.

"Well, as Rebecca knows, I am the one who suggested that she go to therapy. I was very concerned initially about her spacing out and her general lack of drive. She had no interest in anything aside from the guys she dated. Then she would get rid of them. I didn't like what I was seeing, but I'm her roommate, not her therapist. Lately, I must say, I've seen a change for the better." Rebecca looked over at Hannah and smiled, patting her on the knee. "We are having normal conversations, and Rebecca is laughing more than before."

"What was she like beforehand?"

"If I were to sum her up in one word—MOODY! I suffer from depression, so I was able to relate to the times she wanted to be by herself. But then she would get irritable and yell, not necessarily at me, but at everyone else, even the salespeople who call her phone..."

I was thinking about how many "scam likely" phone calls I get every day and how I am tempted to answer and give them a piece of my mind.

Hannah continued, "Last night, Rebecca talked about auditioning for a show and she actually made contact with the company running the show. In the past, she would talk about doing stuff, but would never do it. That was majorly major!"

I looked over at Rebecca who was watching Hannah talk. "Rebecca, that is terrific. In fact, I am really happy with everything I am hearing. How does it feel to hear such great things?"

"Thank you, Hannah. I really appreciate you coming and sharing that with Dr. Lasson and me."

Rebecca seemed to have mastered this skill.

"You see, Dr. Lasson. She was never able to just take a compliment for what it was. She used to say I was complimenting her just to flatter her."

"Well, I am certainly glad to hear from you, Hannah. You have been a caring friend and, I believe, part of the reason why Rebecca is doing so well."

"Can I ask you something, Dr. Lasson?"

"Sure."

"Rebecca mentioned that you discussed attempting to meet her real dad. My concern is that she's made so much progress that I'm worried about it causing a setback. Are you concerned about that?"

"Yes, Hannah. Rebecca can tell you what possible disappointments she is expecting, but what specifically are you most concerned about?"

Rebecca looked over at Hannah, curious what she was thinking.

Hannah looked down at her lap and then looked back up. "Rebecca can be a good friend, at times. We can laugh and talk about personal stuff and just be comfortable with each other. But when she gets into one of her moods, it's like being a prisoner in your own house. The past month or so has been the most stable I have seen Rebecca. I haven't had to worry much about who I was coming home to. There have not been any random weird guys over, and we are just spending quality time together. I just worry about her mood turning ugly again."

Rebecca looked over at Hannah and grabbed hold of her hand. In a soft voice said, "Hannah, I am so sorry I put you through all those ups and downs. I know I have not always been the easiest person to live with, but I am working hard on myself.

Dr. Lasson is really helping me see how I can change the way I think and live a more positive and healthy life."

Hannah leaned into Rebecca and rested her head in her lap with tears coming from her eyes. Rebecca stroked her hair and remained silent. After a few minutes, Hannah sat up and said, "another major thing is that Rebecca is more comfortable just having quiet time. The chaos has calmed down."

"I am certainly happy to hear how well Rebecca is doing, and I am here to guide her on her journey. I would not want anything to jeopardize her progress. Rebecca, what are you anticipating in meeting with your father?"

"Well…for one thing, he might not even be around. Secondly, who says he wants to meet with me? Thirdly, let's say things don't go well and I have some sort of relapse?"

With that, Hannah said, "That is what I am most concerned about."

I let the concerns sink in as I sat back and admired Hannah's concern and steadfast friendship that she and Rebecca shared.

We finished the session after I suggested that they go home and think about how they wanted to go about having this reunion, or the closure of a chapter in Rebecca's life. Rebecca said she would speak to her mother and first see if it would even be possible.

I figured that would be the topic of our next session, so when Rebecca came into the next session smiling from ear-to-ear, I was curious to hear what happened.

Rebecca had made so much progress, but given her history, the glimmer of hope that things would work out in her favor was something I thought of as a far-fetched possibility. I was surprised at myself and disappointed by my pessimism. My role was simply to go with the flow and let the cards fall the way they were meant to.

So, when Rebecca told me what had transpired with her meeting with her mother, I had to quickly switch modes to match her emotions. She was happy, and I had no right to not be happy for her. Apparently, her mother had also been on a quest to find the other half that helped produce Rebecca. She had done much research and tracked down a man living only thirty miles away in Howard County, Maryland. She found a picture of him on a LinkedIn profile and brought it to an agency that helps people find long-lost friends and relatives. The agency had developed software that could digitally produce a lifelike picture of someone as they would appear when they were much younger. The picture of the man her mother had been with that night was almost an exact match. Rebecca was so excited by this new development, yet she was curious why her mother was searching for the biological father. Her mother revealed to Rebecca that she had been in therapy herself, trying to redevelop a sense of trust and wanted to connect with Rebecca in a more meaningful way. The timing of their mutual quest could not have been more serendipitous, so my faith that something positive would come out of this quest was restored.

I felt that Rebecca was in a pretty good place at this point. She was enrolled in some classes at a community college, she had been chosen for a role at a local theater company, and she was developing more meaningful relationships. Plus, she had an amazing friend in Hannah. I was fully in step with Rebecca at this point as she had lost the staring persona and now was one of my most enjoyable clients to work with. Her motivation was nothing short of admirable.

For myself, I personally felt Charlie's presence before, during, and after each session. I kept hearing him in the background saying, "Loosen up, Jonathan. Loosen up, Jonathan." I found myself beginning to trust again after a few years of being on guard all the time and having developed a rigidity that I was not proud of. I did not like the Jonathan of that period of distrust. I spoke to Charlie about the countertransference I experienced during my sessions with Rebecca. I decided that I needed to do something for myself, so I arranged to hang out and paint pottery with my daughter—an activity we both enjoy. I painted a saucer with a beach motif and the word "relax" written on top. Whenever I put my coffee down on the saucer, I was reminded of what I needed to do more of. I realized that I was in somewhat of a healing process of my own, and I was grateful to my friends and family for reminding me to take the proverbial chill pill.

During one session, Rebecca told me about her conversation with her mother. I was thrilled to hear how Rebecca and her mother were connecting on such a meaningful level. During that conversation, Rebecca and her mother decided that her mother should be the one to initiate contact and the possibility of a reunion with Ron, the probable biological father to Rebecca. I thought that would be the best approach as well.

A week later, during our next session, Rebecca came in and said that her mom had received a response from Ron and that he was indeed interested in meeting Rebecca. He had remembered his very brief relationship with Rebecca's mom and said that he always wondered what had become of this lady. He had no idea that their one night together had produced a child. Rebecca's mom was very surprised at how refined a man Ron was during their conversation. He had apparently straightened his life up after a brief marriage to a woman with severe mental health issues. He didn't have any children and was actually excited to hear that he had fathered a child. Rebecca wanted to see what this man looked like, so her mother showed her his profile on LinkedIn. Rebecca was surprised to see a handsome man with a bright smile. The most astonishing feature that caught Rebecca off guard was his full head of red hair.

The reunion was arranged for the following week at a park in Columbia, Maryland. Rebecca, as excited as she was to meet her biological father after all these years, disclosed that she was intentionally playing down the reunion. I was impressed that she was mentally processing everything that had taken place and was about to take place. I recognized this as I realized how excited I was about this reunion.

The session that followed the reunion was one which I will not soon forget. Rebecca was very animated and told me about her father in great detail. They met for over two hours and found that they had much in common aside from their red hair. The reunion was successful. We processed her feelings about her father and discussed weaning off of therapy.

As our sessions came to a close, we spent the final meeting reflecting on how far she had come. Filled with emotion, Rebecca cried tears of joy at the progress she made during our work together. She had learned many things. She learned how to be present, how to take a compliment, and how to give a compliment. She went on to pursue acting and has embarked on writing her first book.

My own reflections were primarily an offshoot of how I worked through my own ambivalence in treating Rebecca. I promised to be kinder to myself and stick with what I was good at. I realized that there is nothing wrong with being fond of a client. This is a good type of countertransference. I was learning to get over some of the trust issues I had and was thankful to have Charlie as a colleague and mentor. Although the population of my clientele has changed over the recent years, I am open to new challenges and opportunities for growth. I thank Rebecca for allowing me to help her on her journey.

MILTON'S HONOR

*The one who plants trees, knowing that he will never
sit in their shade has at least started to understand
the meaning of life,*
—Rabindranath Tagore in *Legacy*

Ordinarily, I am not on the receiving end of referrals for
elderly clients. So when I do get a referral for an
elderly client, I am usually pretty excited. As a person
who never got to meet either his maternal or paternal
grandfather, I have tended to gravitate toward grandfather
figures throughout my life, even to this day. I find them to be
fascinating historians—full of wonderful, real-life stories that
paint a portrait of a person inside a tapestry of beautifully woven
family history. I often refer to these people as the unsung heroes.
Everybody has a story, and some need to be told.

A friend of mine recently sent me the story of a man who was
referred to by the locals as "Old Ed," or sometimes "Crazy Old
Ed." Every Friday night Old Ed would take a stroll down to the
pier holding a bucket of shrimp. He would stare off into the sky,
seemingly lost in thought. Finally, hundreds of white dots would
appear in the sky. As those white dots became larger and larger,
they took the form of seagulls. The seagulls would hover over

Ed's head, and he would throw the shrimp in their direction. As the seagulls ate the shrimp, Ed could be heard saying to the birds, "Thank you, thank you." He would do this until the gulls finished all the shrimp he had brought in his bucket.

To the onlooker, this man feeding and talking to the seagulls seemed like just one more crazy old man. But if you knew his story, your outlook would change.

This man's real name was Edward Vernon Rickenbacker. He was the founder of Eastern Airlines, an American Fighter Ace, and a race car driver. During World War II, Rickenbacker's bomber ran into some trouble and had to divert its route and ended up in a remote area of the Central Pacific Ocean. Rickenbacker and eight of his friends were lost at sea for twenty-four days. On the eighth day, their food supply was just about gone until a seagull landed on Rickenbacker's head. He quickly grabbed the bird, and then divided his captured food among his comrades and used some as bait to catch fish. This continued until they were eventually rescued. All but one of the men survived.

Now, we can understand what Old Ed was muttering to the seagulls in his later years. He was giving thanks to the species that kept him and his mates alive when death was knocking at his door.

I tell this story to my children from time to time to illustrate two themes. One is to give thanks to all creatures and also to understand that everyone has a story.

Milton Sherman also had a story.

Milton was referred to me by his wife, Gloria, because it appeared as if he was experiencing the early stages of dementia. He seemed to be forgetting things, like bringing in the groceries from the car—or forgetting to even bring them home from the store after he bought them. He began forgetting names of people in their condo development and would often get lost while out on his walks. Gloria had taken away the car keys from Milton, which made him depressed. Milton had always been in pretty good shape and would work out at the gym even in his late seventies. Although he had excellent upper body strength from his time spent in the military, lately his knees prevented him from participating in many activities at the gym, which increased his depression. For Milton, the gym was not just a place to exercise; it was his primary source of socialization.

My first step was to conduct a neuropsychological assessment on Milton. The assessment was rather extensive, so I broke it up into four different days, as Milton would tire quickly. At the beginning and end of each assessment session, Milton would give me a military salute and a firm handshake. I had lots of respect and admiration for Milton and, even though I had not been in the military, I would salute in return. It was Milton's way of honoring those he'd lost and the country he'd served with devotion. I would not deny him that honor.

The assessment revealed that Milton was indeed suffering from dementia. His depression index was mild to moderate, depending on the time of the day. Evenings were difficult, and sleep did not come easily for Milton. He would wake up in cold sweats and suffer severe night terrors. At times, he would wake up and stand, as if in a military procession, saluting some imaginary officer. Each time I met with Milton during the assessment phase, he would recount a story—the same exact one with the same exact details about a military buddy—that he found comical. Gloria, who attended the sessions with him, would remind him that he had already told me the story, but Milton would just nod and say, "It's a great story." (Milton wanted to honor his comrades and would write large checks to veteran's associations—a problem for the family once Milton lost his ability to manage their finances. Eventually Gloria and her son concocted a solution: they gave Milton outdated checks from an account that no longer existed so Milton could continue his ritual of writing a check out to his buddies.)

Following the assessment, Milton became my client. Milton was a devoted and doting husband. He wanted to make Gloria happy, so he consented to therapy. Our main goal was to lift him out of his depressive state. During the assessment phase, I had not really gotten to know Milton very well, as he was not able to produce many responses due to the dementia. Dementia often is associated with hypothyroidism, which can cause patients to present with psychotic and depressive symptoms. Milton's psychotic symptoms were not severe, but the depression seemed to be getting progressively worse, especially now that he no longer had his "set of wheels," which was how he referred to his beloved Buick. There were also some noticeable changes in brain mass, as well as cerebrospinal fluid that changed the levels of proteins that form abnormal brain deposits. This is usually a precursor to Alzheimer's disease.

In my formulation of a treatment plan, I refused to treat Milton as a *patient* with Alzheimer's, but rather as a *client* who was going through some difficult life changes. In fact, I did not look at Milton as a patient at all. Part of me saw in Milton what I envisioned as the grandfather I never met. Putting aside the PET scans and the results from his neuropsychological assessment, I went along with my countertransference (finally, I felt I was getting to know the grandfather I never knew) and my desire to learn more about Milton's life. After consulting with the supervising psychologist, we both agreed that it would be a good idea to engage Milton in a biographical memory task. This, in essence, was Milton recounting his life story. Indeed, these sessions became the highlight of Milton's week and, in some ways, the highlight of my week.

As is often the case when conducting therapy with older clients, a family member is brought in to fill in the gaps that the client misses. Gloria proved to be a wonderful historian. At times during our sessions, Milton would stop mid-sentence and turn to Gloria and hold her hand. She would remind him of the word or the name of the person he was thinking of. There was a twinkle in Milton's eye that could melt anyone's heart, and it was obvious that the love that Milton and Gloria shared was one of passion and commitment.

Gloria was also an excellent co-therapist. When Milton was feeling down, Gloria would lift him up by watching numerous episodes of M*A*S*H and Three's Company. Even though she had watched these shows numerous times, she knew it had a healing effect on Milton's depression. Gloria also possessed a beautiful singing voice and had performed in many local shows. She would sing to Milton when she noticed him feeling down. Milton's musical inclination was restricted to playing in a couple of bands when he was younger. Nonetheless, he seemed to appreciate the healing effects of watching comedy and listening to Gloria's melodious voice, as evidenced by his depression inventories that were charted daily.

Gloria and Milton were blessed with three children: two sons and a daughter. They now had thirteen grandchildren, who each brought much joy to the Sherman household. Gloria and Milton doted over their children and made sure that each of them received the best education and extracurricular activities in the interest of the child. Mark, the oldest of the children, was an accomplished physician and lived in closest proximity to Gloria and Milton. He would visit every Sunday and take Milton and his own children to Oriole games and local cultural events. Cheryl had Milton's engineering genes and worked as a civil engineer, and the two of them had many discussions about the trade. Milton was particularly fond of Cheryl for this reason, as well as the fact that she was his only daughter. When Cheryl was considering marriage, Milton interrogated her fiancé to make sure that she had chosen well. At first, Cheryl was upset with her father for asking very personal questions about her fiancé, Lawrence, but admitted that it felt good that her dad was looking out for her. The youngest son, Benny, was, as Milton and Gloria put it, the family clown. Always good for a practical joke, Benny had been a frequent flyer at the principal's office during his school years. He eventually went into sports journalism as a career, and Milton loved the time he and Benny would spend together talking sports and occasionally Baltimore politics, about which Benny had many strong opinions. It was a very loving family. During the high holidays, the Shermans would pile into Milton's Buick and go to the synagogue to pray together. They spent many holidays and birthdays together, and Milton remembered some of the details of these special occasions.

Milton had served in World War II as a decorated general. At first, Milton had been involved more on the technical side due to his knowledge of machinery and technology. Milton did not want to limit his military experience to the engineering side, so he demanded (his words) that he be deployed and serve as an active soldier. He was involved in some ground action and had, in fact, saved the lives of several of his comrades. Milton earned a Purple Heart for his bravery. Milton's squad came under enemy fire from all sides; he detonated an explosive in just the right spot at just the right time to avoid a certain ambush.

Milton remembered Emperor Hirohito surrendering in a radio address. After the war, he met Gloria in Gloria's hometown of Baltimore. Back in those days, Baltimore was a bustling American city that took great pride in its ability to produce many items necessary for the military to continue its offensive, if it were to become necessary. Milton's competence in many areas of technology landed him a job as a civil engineer in a reputable engineering firm. I confess that my knowledge of engineering is rudimentary at best, but Milton had a way of explaining some of the basics so that even I could understand the nature of his work.

Milton's memory had much to do with Baltimore in the 1950s. He had memories of going to Hess' shoe store and getting lollipops for his children, while Gloria would sing songs about lollipops. He remembered going to all the delicatessens on Lombard Street, which was known as "deli row." He especially loved going to Memorial Stadium to watch the Baltimore Orioles. The Shermans lived in the Forest Park area of Baltimore until the 1970s, Milton recalled, when they moved to an area of Baltimore County called Pikesville. Milton was an avid fan of the Baltimore Orioles and the football team at the time, the Baltimore Colts. He remembered the great quarterback, Johnny Unitas, and Orioles pitcher, Jim Palmer. He would imitate the announcer, Chuck Thompson, especially when he would yell out, "Ain't the beer cold!" and "Go to war Miss Agnes!" Because of my own familiarity with Chuck Thompson and the Baltimore sports teams, we hit it off in therapy. I certainly felt more at ease talking sports than civil engineering. I cherished these biographical memory sessions and began seeing some degree of improvement in Milton's depressive symptoms.

Milton continued to have sleep difficulties and would at times wake up from a nightmare saying, "Yes Sir!" Gloria was concerned and asked me if there was anything I could do. Apparently, the sleep medications were having a paradoxical effect on Milton, so I advised his doctor to wean him off while I tried hypnotherapy on Milton. Milton proved to be an excellent candidate for hypnosis and Gloria was helpful in picking out musical selections to help with at-home inductions into a pseudo-hypnotic state. She chose old Jewish tunes without words that Milton remembered from his childhood. After a few weeks of hypnosis and a gradual weaning off his sleep meds, Milton was sleeping soundly again. Still, his memory continued to deteriorate, and the brain scans were not looking promising. His most recent scan showed more buildup of neurofibrillary tangles in his brain, which indicated that the disease was progressing. I started becoming very angry at Alzheimer's for what it had done to several of my relatives, as well as to what it was doing to Milton.

I was devoted to Milton. I understood that his neurocognitive deficits would continue to worsen, but I was determined to find out as much as I could about Milton's life and how he remained so positive. I wanted to learn the story of this remarkable man who had touched many lives. What was amazing was that Milton's depressive episodes did not involve any sense of bitterness or negativity toward others. It was all directed inward. He would make self-deprecating remarks about what he could no longer do and, sadly, at times questioned the point of living.

Gloria came to one session somewhat more nervous than usual. She explained that the neurologist had given her a bleak report about Milton's last exam. I explained to Gloria that although medically Milton may not be looking very good, his good spirit was prolonging his ability to rehabilitate some neurons. I was not really sure this was entirely accurate from a scientific perspective, but it was important for Gloria to hear that so she would continue to advocate and help Milton through his final years.

Milton's greatness was showing at a time when most people had written him off. He recorded some of his memories when he was first diagnosed with primary progressive aphasia. In turn, Gloria had them transcribed so their children would be able to read them someday. Gloria began to invite me to her home to visit Milton, as he was losing his ability to navigate the stairs and had already suffered from several falls. I did not mind going to the Sherman home to provide therapy and help him get some sleep (which had greatly improved since our initial meeting). In fact, as soon as I pulled up and walked through the door, Gloria would joke with Milton that the anesthesiologist was coming.

Regaining memory functioning is not something I expect from the elderly. During one visit, I was surprised at some of the things Milton was telling me. For example, he recalled a specific event when he had been in synagogue with his father. He recalled going to what he referred to as the "Shul in the Park." A *shul* is the Yiddish term for a synagogue. I knew exactly which synagogue he was referring to because my father-in-law had served as the congregation's rabbi for about ten years. The synagogue, which was featured in Barry Levinson's film *Liberty Heights*, was an iconic synagogue that boasted famous Baltimoreans when the Baltimore Jewish community flourished back in the 1940s and 1950s. To this day, when I drive past the synagogue, which is right across the street from the Baltimore Zoo, I imagine Milton sitting with his father in the old pews listening to the liturgy and sermons.

Milton informed me that he was a shul-goer as well as a shul-lover. He remembered sitting with his father and singing the tunes of Lecha Dodi on Friday night and then going home to the smells of his mother's chicken matzo ball soup and potato kugel, two staples in many Jewish homes. He would watch his mother light the Shabbat candles while covering her eyes, which she explained helped her concentrate on a prayer she said for the welfare of her children and husband. This event had made a major impression on Milton. What was amazing was that he had very specific sensory memories from the house on Friday night, including the song, the aroma of his mother's cooking, his father's three-piece suit, and his mother's floral gown that she wore every Friday night. I asked Milton if we could sing the Lecha Dodi together (hoping I knew the tune, which, thankfully, turned out to be one of the more common ones). To see Milton's glee while singing was delightful. He seemed to be teleporting back to those times when he would sing these familiar tunes with his father. Those visits with Milton were very special to me.

Consulting with Milton's doctors was one of my weekly tasks so I could help inform Gloria and the children of what to expect. His memory began deteriorating at a more rapid pace, and there was mention of contacting hospice to help with the process. Gloria would not hear of it, although her three children felt that this was the most realistic option, given the toll Milton's condition was taking on their mother. Gloria began having an awful time falling asleep and asked for the "anesthesiologist" to work his magic on her. Of course, I obliged. When Gloria's sessions were over, I asked if we could meet with her children. She already knew what I was going to say, but our connection was one based on trust that I only had the family's best interest in mind. She knew the affection I had for Milton and asked me if I loved him. I responded, "Very much," with a tear in my eye. With that interaction, she agreed to a meeting.

I prepped Milton and Gloria's children about the meeting where we would discuss end-of-life options, including hospice care. Mark, Cheryl, and Benny agreed on a time and a place to meet with their mother and me.

At our meeting we discussed what hospice is, and what hospice is not. I thank my wife for educating me about hospice so I could sound somewhat intelligent and informed about what hospice could offer. At the time of this meeting, Milton's disease was progressing rapidly, and the family agreed to home hospice.

I was able to secure a wonderful rabbi to assist the family in spiritual planning and a nurse who was familiar with Jewish customs, particularly when it came to end-of-life issues. We had formed a very collaborative team, and the family was very grateful for the efforts of all involved. Milton was in the comfort of his own home, with children and grandchildren coming over on a more frequent basis. I tried to be there as often as possible as I cherished these family moments. Although the Shermans were not my own family, I began looking at them as family. I established bonds with all three children as we navigated the spiritual and emotional complexities that occur as life in this world wanes and a new chapter begins.

As Milton's memory had become limited to only memories of music, my last few sessions with Milton were that of music therapy. Milton seemed to relax most when I would sing to him. Gloria would sometimes hold his hand and sing along, which relaxed him even more. His grandchildren were not as familiar with the tunes, so I lent them a CD to learn some of the songs we were singing. The oldest grandchild, Molly, who was closest to Milton, picked up quickly and would take over singing duties when Gloria was too tired. This was true palliative care. The whole family was involved, and Milton remained in his own home. As I would take leave of Milton, he would look at me and offer a soldier's salute. I would salute him in return, wondering about the profound impact his military service had on him, even during his final days.

When Milton passed away, I was on vacation with my family. I received a voicemail from Molly saying that he'd passed peacefully. She wanted to thank me and informed me of the funeral plans. I returned from my vacation and although I missed the funeral, I attended the shiva—a seven-day period of mourning when family and friends visit the relatives of the deceased. It is part of the Jewish end-of-life process and a time to share memories of the deceased. When Gloria saw me enter the home, she quickly got up and smiled. She introduced me to a couple of her friends as her husband's *anesthesiologist*. I sat with Mark, Cheryl, and Benny and led the traditional memorial prayer service upon Gloria's request. That was my honor to Milton.

Following my shiva visit, I sat in my car and took in the sights. My appreciation for what I had in life needed some work. Seeing Milton's family and having the honor of working with Milton had opened my eyes to the small things that I sometimes took for granted. The ability to speak and think and remember information are the products of such incredible neural complexity, a complexity that I, admittedly, take for granted.

As advances in therapies for Alzheimer's disease increase, I hope that those suffering from neurocognitive decline will be able to reverse the effects that impact so many. In June of 2021 the FDA approved the use of a new drug called Aduhelm for the treatment of some forms of Alzheimer's. This drug is an anti-amyloid antibody that works by removing amyloid from the brain, a substance which builds up over time. This is a promising advancement, and I remain optimistic that it will help many people. In the meantime, my job will be to continue to show patience and creativity in working with this special and greatly misunderstood population. They certainly deserve the same honor and respect as those whose faculties are intact.

Milton still lives inside my heart and soul. I still feel very connected to him. Working with Milton has made me a more spiritual person. I have experienced many humbling moments since Milton's passing. My time spent in shul has become more special and precious. My children all know me now as an avid shul-goer. During the COVID-19 pandemic when all synagogues had to shutter their doors, I had a difficult time adjusting to the idea of praying at home instead of going to the synagogue. Now that the synagogues have reopened, I feel much more uplifted by the communal praying. When I sing the Lecha Dodi, my mind often drifts to thoughts of Milton. He is no longer among the living; however, Milton's story will endure for eternity.

TAYLOR MADE

All the variety, all the charm, all the beauty
of life are made up of light and shade.
—Leo Tolstoy

Working with children always brings exhilaration and challenges. As mentioned in my other stories of working with children, children don't come on their own to the therapy room. They are usually escorted by an adult, namely a parent or two. So, it is safe to say that one major difference between working with children versus adults is that with adults there is the assumption that the adult coming to see you is capable of making decisions without any other family members present. There are times, however, where you question the decision-making of the adults who bring their children in for therapy.

Taylor was eleven years old when she came to see me for the first time. Prior to my initial session with Taylor, I spoke briefly with Taylor's mother who described her as a bright and precocious girl who did not have many friends. Her goal for Taylor was to learn better social skills. Mom provided me with a previous psychological assessment that was conducted by a school psychologist when Taylor was seven. Taylor had an IQ that was in the superior range of cognitive ability. Her behavior rating scales filled out by her teachers at the time painted a different picture of Taylor. Taylor was described as oppositional and socially off. She had an elevated score in a domain known as "atypicality." The school psychologist suggested that it was possible that Taylor was on the "spectrum," which means she may have some degree of autism.

I agreed to see Taylor first with her mother to get a feel for how they interacted with each other and then would spend the last twenty minutes of the session just with Taylor. While Taylor and Mom were with me, there was not much that was out of the ordinary. Taylor sat and listened and from time to time would correct her mother. Her mother would simply say, "That's correct" or "Yes, you are right, Taylor. That is more of an accurate description of what happened." Many kids who come to meet with a stranger for the first time demonstrate some sense of anxiety. Taylor did not show any anxiety whatsoever, which I immediately jotted down on my notepad.

Taylor looked a little older than her stated age of eleven. She was tall and lanky and wore a pair of glasses that gave her that "brainy child" look. She had short blond hair and piercing blue eyes. She rarely smiled during that first session. She spoke in a measured way, as if she were reading off a teleprompter. Mom had already mentioned that she and the father lived separately and that he was not an active part of their lives. She said that Taylor's father had been diagnosed with Asperger's Syndrome, and he rarely had normal interactions with Taylor or her younger brother, Tyler. Taylor's father worked as an engineer for a large firm in Baltimore. He had some custodial rights but would often choose to skip his weekends that he would be allowed to have Taylor stay with him, an arrangement which seemed to be fine with Mom and Taylor. I tried making some small talk with Taylor, but she seemed disinterested. So, I took a chance at small talk based on a previous comment made by her mother about her interest in weather. I asked her if she thought it would be scary to chase tornadoes. I have seen people who love to chase and film active tornadoes. When I asked this question, Taylor's blue eyes grew wide, and she said that she would love to chase a tornado. We spoke for a couple more minutes, and I asked Taylor if she would be interested in teaching me a little more about weather. She gave me a thumbs up and walked out to the waiting room.

There are things that thrill some people and not others. I am not enthralled with weather or tornadoes. However, since I made the offer to Taylor, it behooved me to familiarize myself with earth science so I could sound somewhat intelligent when I next met with Taylor. I was about to look up some information about weather stuff when Taylor's mother called me and asked me why I was asking her daughter to tutor me in earth science. I calmly explained to her that this was simply a means to get to know Taylor better without getting into emotionally loaded topics. She continued to assert that she was not paying me to act as a tutor. Again, I tried to explain to Mom my intention, which is common—or should be common—for psychologists who work with children. She still seemed upset and warned me that she would not continue to send Taylor if I did not address her lack of friends. I explained that therapy at this stage is more of a "getting to know you" process. I felt like I was getting to know Mom better and saw that she could go from calm to explosive in a flash. She agreed to one more session and then she would reevaluate. I said, "fair enough" and the conversation ended.

I realized that therapy with Taylor would be more challenging because of Mom's unrealistic expectations of therapy outcomes and Taylor's need to be spoken to like an adult. I agreed with the past assessment and the suspicions that Taylor possibly fell on the "spectrum." But it did not appear like a classic case of autism. I was thinking that perhaps Taylor was trying to escape something more psychological by hiding behind this adult persona. The challenges would be multifaceted in working with Taylor. First, Mom was clearly a difficult person to work with. Second, I was unsure if I would have access to Dad. Third, were the suspicions of autism spectrum disorder accurate? Lastly, my understanding of earth science was rudimentary at best and my interest in furthering my education with Taylor was just not there. I went back home and saw my daughter's textbook on earth science and brought it with me to the kitchen while I made myself a coffee. I opened the textbook and read through a little on the weather section and wondered how people could be so fascinated with this stuff. But then again, I am also interested in things that others are not, and that's how it is for everyone. That's what makes us all unique.

For many years, I have worked with children who were considered to be on the spectrum. The impact it has on the child is usually in the social realm. My colleagues throw around the word *autistic* and, *on the spectrum*, as if they are interchangeable. Many children with autism do not speak and may have severe language impairments. Those children tend to be more classically autistic, and the issues are more apparent earlier on than with children who might be on the spectrum. It has gotten to the point that many diagnosticians label any child who enjoys learning yet appears socially off as being "on the spectrum." I don't always see it that way. That was what made working with

Taylor all the more intriguing. Mom's primary interest in sending Taylor for therapy was to help her develop friendships. My primary interest at the time was to develop familiarity with Taylor and what exactly makes her responsive.

During our follow-up session, I made a concerted effort to ask Taylor about her friends. She said she did not have much of an interest in the kids in school. She then said she had some imaginary friends. We talked about each of these friends as if they were real people. Taylor was more expressive when discussing one particular friend whom she called Logan. She said that Logan could be mean at times, but she thinks he is cool because he reads a lot. This is not the standard operating definition of the word cool for most eleven-year-olds. Taylor was certainly different from typical kids her age, but at least I had broached the subject of friends, so I would have something to report to Mom when we would meet for the last few minutes of our session.

Perhaps it was Mom having to wait in the waiting room for about forty minutes that had calmed her down, or it was what I told her. Now I was getting the more amiable mother of a socially struggling preteen. When I meet with parents toward the end of a session with a child, they are usually looking for some golden nuggets they can take from this person they are paying to help their child. I informed Mom that Taylor was indeed bright, and that she did have friends. It was just that they were mostly embedded in her imagination. In order to merge the imaginary with the real, it would be a good idea to have Taylor enroll in an after-school science camp. I had recently taken one of my children who is also fascinated with science to a Nature Center in Baltimore and recommended that Mom do the same. In fact, there was a program the next night with a focus on the planets. The director of the program had a very expensive telescope that clearly showed the stars and other meteor phenomenon. Mom was impressed that I had addressed the friend issue and also provided her with something practical.

That weekend, Mom called me and left a message for me to call back. When I called her back (twenty minutes later), she seemed surprised by my quick response. After a bit of praise for being responsive, she informed me that Taylor wanted to enroll for all the programs at the center and that she also was excited to meet with me again.

One rule of thumb that I took from a prior supervisor was that the most important thing about being a therapist was to be responsive when a client calls. I've never had much of a problem in that area. I did find this advice ironic coming from this particular supervisor, as he was chronically late for everything. Our supervision sessions were frequently delayed or canceled altogether or he would accept calls during our time together. There was always some excuse, but I just went with the flow and tried to get whatever I could out of him during supervision, which, unfortunately, was not much. (Note to people in supervisory positions: be on time and be present for your supervisees.)

Back to Taylor. Taylor came in for her third session with more of a spring in her step. She spoke about the next planetarium exhibit that she would be attending and asked if I would go with her. I explained to her that it sounded very interesting, but I could not go with her as I was her therapist. I asked her if she met any other kids at the center whom she liked and she told me about a really nice nine-year-old boy whom she described as a genius. They developed a nice relationship and spoke about what they saw at the center. They even exchanged emails. I suggested that perhaps the two of them could go together to the next exhibit. She thought about it and said, "As long as Mom agrees." When I met with Mom, she readily agreed and mentioned that she met the parent of this nine-year-old and she seemed like a decent person. She threw in, "I still wish that Taylor would find friends her own age." Seeing that I was not reacting, she quickly inserted, "But thanks for the suggestion. She seems happier and more occupied."

Taylor was the type of kid who grew on you. We did not share many of the same interests, yet she was interesting. A therapist does not have to have the same interests and should not force themselves to take on similar interests. This is what makes good therapists, great therapists. We need to be chameleons to some degree, adapting and valuing the interests of others. When the client is a child, we again transform into the advisor for the parent and validator of emotions. A strange outcome of my sessions with Taylor was I became more interested in science than ever before. Her passion for earth science was contagious. I don't think I will ever know as much as Taylor about meteorology, and that is perfectly fine. It's not my role. What many modality therapists fail to recognize is that rapport-building takes precedence over whatever therapeutic modality you intend to employ with your client.

Taylor's mother asked if she could join us for the fourth session. As a general rule of thumb, I said I would have to confer with Taylor if that would be okay. Mom put Taylor on the phone and Taylor said it would be fine.

Our next session was scheduled for early in the morning. This was fine for Taylor, as she was an early riser. Taylor and Mom came in together. Taylor had a notepad and a colorful pen with her and a radiant smile on her face, which was unusual, given her typical, more serious facial expressions. I began the session asking Mom why she was interested in meeting together. She said, "To be honest, I just wanted to see how you are able to connect with her. You seem to be able to get her to become more animated, and she actually looks forward to meeting with you." I was surprised that this was her reason to join today and decided to play it safe so I would not assume things that were untrue. So, I asked Taylor to respond to Mom's question.

Taylor thought for a moment and said something profound, which after getting to know her was not really surprising. "I have a theory. Humans, in general, are not very predictable. I like when things make sense, when things are real, when things are predictable. Science makes sense to me, and I decided that I like to teach the things that I know. I also know that I come off as a little weird because of my interests. Dr. Lasson is a very good student even though he is old. He seems interested in learning about tornadoes and earthquakes. He is also more predictable than most Homo sapiens. No one else seems to care much." She looked over at me and smiled.

Mom became slightly defensive and said, "I care about you, honey. And I am your mother! I just want you to make friends with people your own age."

"Mom. People my age don't appreciate me. In fact, they make fun of me and bully me. I never told you, but a few months ago, two girls grabbed me while I was in the bathroom and blocked the stall. They kept throwing wet toilet paper at me and calling me all sorts of bad names."

This was the first time I saw Taylor express such emotion. She had never told me about this event either. Mom was furious and made the mistake of asking her, "Why didn't you tell me?"

The appropriate response would have been, "Taylor, I am so sorry this happened to you." Maybe a hug or some reassurance.

Taylor, reacting to Mom's question of why she'd kept this silent said, "Mom, you would have gone to the principal right away and made sure these girls were punished." Taylor continued, "From a predictability standpoint, that would be a very stupid thing to do. That would only encourage them and get more people to bully me. Why don't you get it?"

There are points of time during the therapy process and particularly during an exchange between two family members, where many therapists are tempted to intervene, trying to clarify what the other is saying. I usually hold back and allow the process to continue without me. Taylor just revealed that she was being bullied at school. Mom reacted with her natural protective instinct but questioned why she wasn't told about it. There are many reasons why children do not disclose abusive behavior or bullying. One reason is that they are really scared of the repercussions of disclosing to a parent and possible overreactions. Taylor was approaching it logically, while Mom was having an emotional reaction.

After a minute, Taylor turned to me and asked me what I thought she should do. I turned it back and asked Taylor, "What makes the most sense to you?"

Without missing a beat, Taylor said, "I don't want my mom to do anything. She always wants to get involved. If I complain about a teacher who I don't feel is a good teacher, my mom will say, 'Well, we need to go to the school and let the principal take care of this teacher.' I think Mom would have the whole staff fired. So, I stopped complaining."

Becoming defensive, Mom turned to Taylor and said, "I would not do that, sweetie. But I want to hear what is going on in school. I want to be part of your life."

This was a familiar scene for me in therapy, especially with children and their parents: finding the balance between appropriate intervention and overstepping on behalf of your children. I surmised something that I confirmed with Mom later on. She had not had an ideal upbringing and her parents had not been involved in her schooling. They ignored her completely when school issues came up. They never attended parent conferences. Mom was subconsciously overcompensating for the lack of proper parental interest by becoming, in Taylor's view, a helicopter parent.

At the next session, I asked Mom to come by herself. My intent was to convey to her what I was seeing, with two hopes and expectations. One was that Mom would understand that she was overcompensating and living vicariously through Taylor. Second was to educate her as to what Taylor really needed at this stage of her life. I wanted Mom to understand that my goal was not to keep Taylor as a long-term client, since it would just take a few adjustments in parenting to get her back on track and reduce Taylor's dependency on me for support and validation.

My objectives were laid out on paper for Mom to read over and this proved very helpful to Mom as she realized that she was, in fact, a good mom. She was using the tools that she had in her parenting toolbox. I validated her and showed her how Taylor is very scientific and operates on a different system of logic than most kids do. I reminded Mom that her goal for Taylor in therapy was to help increase her social network. I spelled out for her the steps she could take as a mother to make this happen. Mom was receptive to my version of "scientific therapy" that worked with Taylor's system of logic and that was more pragmatic for Taylor.

In this day and age where children in schools are filming/recording with smartphones when they do not like something a teacher says or does, parents will often react by intervening and threatening to bring charges against a teacher, school, or system. This might be the intent of an angry child who knows his parents will take their side, but it often backfires. Many people's lives have been ruined through allegations of impropriety based on a child's anger toward a teacher for giving a bad grade or withholding recess or enforcing some other school-based punishment. This causes teachers to be overly cautious and reluctant to give a child the grade they deserve or take a punitive action against a child who has blatantly violated a school rule.

Taylor's mom was also struggling with the idea that Taylor did not seem to have any interest in romantic relationships. Again, Mom was projecting her own expectations onto Taylor. She asked Taylor whether she likes boys or girls and stated that it was okay to like whoever you want. Taylor did not seem to understand what her mother was getting at. So, when Mom asked her more directly if she would ever want to kiss or hug a friend, Taylor did not react well. She asked angrily why she would need to do that and looked at her mother like she was from outer space. Mom expressed to me her fear that Taylor was asexual and had no romantic interests at all. Again, Mom needed to be validated regarding her concerns but also be told that this was her preference at this time of her development. Things could change, but the more Mom insisted, the more distant Taylor would become. Mom dropped the pressure.

In Taylor's case, she was not breaking any rules. She was just different. Mom was trying to take an apple and make it into an orange. Mom was also learning the nature of the therapy relationship. She understood the "rapport first, solution-finding later." She committed to being more patient with the process and agreed to hold back from trying to solve Taylor's problem, because in reality her problems were only exacerbated by Mom trying to swoop in and save the day. This was her doctor's order. It was a tough pill to swallow but a necessary one in order for Taylor to have a successful outcome.

During our last few sessions, Taylor and I role-played social situations in which she was approached by both negative peers and peers who were interested in her for her vast knowledge and being a generally good kid with different interests

My supervisor validated my approach with both Taylor and her mom. This could be seen as a cut and dry case to most therapists. However, Taylor's case caused me to take some more therapeutic risks when the time was ripe for intervention. Taylor's mom came in with an agenda, but Taylor had no agenda. Once in therapy, we created the agenda that would both pacify Mom and provide Taylor with more opportunities for social interaction with same-age peers. In retrospect, I can't think of anything I would have done differently, other than to establish a connection with her father.

Many therapists are quick to place their clients in a box. I primarily refer to the people I see as clients rather than patients for that reason. Patients typically have a diagnosis that helps the doctor understand their symptomatology without making them sound stiff. Therapists must realize that the people they see are malleable. To one therapist, Taylor would be on the spectrum, whereas another therapist would simply say "she is a bit quirky."

I prefer the latter as it makes the diagnosis more subjective as it should be obvious that "quirky" is not a clinical term. I would not like it if someone labeled me with a diagnosis as that would suggest that people cannot change. I don't believe that competent therapists would state that people cannot change. People may be different, but life would be pretty darn boring if everyone were the same! In Taylor's case, she was "Taylor-made" to be exactly who she was—Taylor.

FINDING JASON

*A journey of a thousand miles begins
with a single step.*
—Lao Tzu

In my first book, *The Guilt Trap and Other Tales of Psychotherapy*, I recounted the story of an angry teenager who was able to come to grips with his home and school life. I used an unorthodox approach in dealing with that client, sharing an interest in his music and meeting him on the boardwalk of Miami Beach. Eventually he became quite successful, and we have kept in contact with each other from time to time over the years. I also mentioned that "angry teenagers" tend to be my favorite population to work with as a therapist. That has not changed.

Jason was another of my angry teen clients, although he was no longer officially a teen. Jason did not start as an actual client of mine as there were a couple of hurdles I had to circumvent as you will soon see. Jason's mother had a friend whose nephew was a former client of mine, so she recommended me as a therapist. I had met with Jason's parents for a Zoom session and listened while they bemoaned the fate of their "pothead, drug-addicted son." It was mostly the mother doing the talking, oftentimes comparing Jason with his five other siblings who seemed "perfectly content" with their family. Jason was just turning twenty years old at the time and that posed a challenge for me. Since he was over eighteen, he would need to sign his own consent for me to work with him. The other problem was that his parents did not know where he was.

One of my therapeutic pet peeves is that I don't like working with invisible people. Another pet peeve is that I prefer to meet my clients face to face as opposed to via Zoom or Google Meet. But when I first began working with the family, I was quarantined at home with most of the world as the COVID-19 pandemic raged on. A third pet peeve of mine is that I do not like to treat people who are actively using drugs. Jason's parents' description of him being a pothead did not make him a very alluring client. After some deliberation and sympathy due to the pandemic, I made an exception in Jason's case, as his parents insisted that it was a "life and death" situation.

Over the years, I have made connections with those who have seen the underbelly of an otherwise friendly, functional community. I asked one of my contacts where the "guys" hang out these days. I was told of two possible locations. I gambled and decided on the one closer to my office. After years of working with different populations in different neighborhoods, my fear level has lessened. Most of my friends would never dare venture into such areas and are surprised when I tell them where I stop to get gas. (Tip for the daring: gas tends to be cheapest at stations that neighbor a bail bondsman and a liquor store.)

The first apartment complex I was referred to by my "informant" led me straight to Jason. Jason's parents had given me several pictures of him in varying poses and forms of attire.

Although he put on a tough exterior, I saw him as a young man who just needed to establish his unique sense of self. It sounds corny when I describe kids that way, but it works in reframing a persona.

You did not have to be a toxicologist to know in which apartment Jason would most likely be found. I walked to the door that led to the stench. I was wearing what I would typically wear to work, and the neighbors were obviously not used to seeing someone like me in their part of the hood. I did not intend to stay for a long time. After knocking for what seemed to be minutes, a young man with long curly hair and glazed-over eyes came to the door, which was barely attached to its hinges. After his formal greeting of "Who the hell are you?" I introduced myself and asked to speak with Jason. "Are you his father or something?" Mr. Longhair asked.

"Or something," I responded. It became obvious that he did not want me to come in, so I asked if he could send Jason outside the apartment.

"Are you a cop?" he asked.

"Do you get many cops coming to your door wearing one of these?" I asked, pointing to the yarmulke on my head.

"I guess not," Mr. Longhair responded. The next thing I heard was some rumbling and a combination of boys' and girls' voices coming from inside the apartment.

"I'll just wait outside," I said.

A few minutes later, a tall, handsome young man came out looking both ways until he rested his gaze on me. "Whadda ya want?" Jason asked. It was obvious from the pictures that this was Jason, even though he had no shirt on and was now sporting a goatee. Standing at six foot three, Jason had me looking up at him from my five-foot-nine vantage point.

"I came here because your parents and siblings are concerned about you." I knew ahead of time the type of response such a proclamation would elicit. I braced for it, and it came, with multiple expletives. Most were directed toward his mother. I have learned that kids who fall through rough times, as much as the father is an important figure in their development, the subject of much of the resentment is aimed at the mother. This could be due to a lack of attention given in favor of the favorite child, the mother's arguing with the father and finger pointing to the father as the catalyst to the child's downfall, and the general expectations of nurturing that a child feels should come more naturally to mothers. This is all deeply subconscious, but it often comes out in therapy. (I guess Freud was right about some things.)

Jason finally completed his brief tirade and asked me what I did. I told him I was a therapist. I find it best to be up front at the outset and take it from there. Individuals like Jason don't like to be played with. So if I tried something silly such as saying that I was looking for some good pot or I was looking for an actor for a new film featuring drug addicted teens, I would not realistically be able to follow through with the charade.

"What kind of therapist are you?" Jason asked. Fair question.

"I work with all sorts of people. I try my best to help people lead a more functional life."

Jason looked back into the apartment, which I was still not given an invitation to enter. Not that I wanted to. A young lady with multiple hair colors emerged and stood next to Jason. She had lots of fake jewelry on and was vaping in a demonstrative way. "Is that your dad?" she asked.

"No," Jason said.

"Is he a cop?"

"No. Go get me a beer. Want one?" Jason asked me.

"No thanks," I replied. "Is there somewhere else we can talk?" I asked.

"Where did you have in mind?" was his reply.

"I have an office not too far from here. We do not have to talk right now. Think about it."

Jason looked me up and down, trying to figure out if I was a threat or just some caring man who was trying to help. Dismissing the threat possibility, he asked for my number and said, "I'll call you. But can we get some food?"

"Not a problem." I took his order: fire slammers, burgers, and fries. Once again, he said he would call me. I think he was more motivated to have some good food than actually having an intense therapy session to explore his unconscious inner conflicts.

Leaving the apartment and neighborhood, I stopped to get some gas and placed a call to his parents, telling them that I had made an initial introduction. "Was he smoking?" was their first question. That was the least of my concerns for Jason, but that seemed front and center of their concerns. They were obviously out to lunch. I felt like asking, "Smoking what?" but knew better than to ask that to a semi-grieving family. I realized that I would need to spend lots of time educating this family about the realities of Jason's world.

Meeting with the family the following week, I explained to them approximately where Jason was shacking up without giving them a specific location. They were pleased to know that he was going to meet with me. They agreed to pay for his meal as long as it was "kosher food." I told them that I would have Jason sign his own documents to consent for therapy and to allow me to drive him in my car. They were happy to let him have this autonomy provided that I only give him kosher food.

I asked them to tell me about the family. Not surprisingly, given my past interaction with the parents, the mother took over the storytelling, punctuating her historical perspective by listing the accomplishments of the other children, most notably the oldest son. The father seemed uninterested in hearing all of this once again and did not comment much. His wife would turn to him, looking for reassurance. He just sat there and did not attempt to correct her. I am pretty sure he had tried that in the past and it had backfired. So, he developed what Martin Seligman described as "learned helplessness," and kept his mouth shut. Jason's mother would frequently take out her cell phone and show me pictures of the other children who were doing "so well."

The oldest son, who was now twenty-four and married with one child and one on the way, was on his way to becoming a scholar who would make a tremendous impact on society because "he is so smart." Throughout the session, she kept referring to how many good friends he associated with. "Stable boys from good families" was all she cared about. She spoke with the conviction that she was always right. Her helpless husband just nodded his head in agreement. She also spoke nonstop. At times, she veered so off track and would hound me with personal questions such as, "Isn't your uncle the law professor? My cousin's daughter just took a class with him. Doesn't your wife give swimming lessons?" I was looking forward to the end of this session and was looking even more forward to meeting up with Jason. As angry as he was, I was far more interested in speaking with my angry client than dealing with his mother.

As they left my office, I heard the mother berating her husband for forgetting to bring the shopping list. It became obvious why much of the animosity was directed toward Jason's mother. During the session, the few times the father spoke, he referred to Jason by his Hebrew name, Yaakov. I have seen this before. Dad was trying to hold on to some glimmer of hope that his son would find his way back to his Jewish roots. I felt bad for this father. He was dealing with many conflicting feelings and a wife that could not be present for the family. I wanted to try and reach the father at some point and meet with him alone. In traditional family therapy sessions, the parents would actively participate in the process. In Jason's case, while his parents should be making adjustments in their parenting, they needed far too much work on their marriage, respect for one another, and communication. I would try to recommend a marriage therapist for them, but right now my focus was on Jason.

Jason turned out to be somewhat responsible. Either that or he was extremely hungry. He reached out to me, and when he asked me what he should be calling me, I told him "Doc" was just fine. We agreed to meet at a bench outside my office.

As the agreed-upon time came, I looked out my office window and saw a motorcycle pull up with Jason sitting behind a shorter, muscular guy with lots of tattoos. Jason patted his driver on the back and made some sort of motion, indicating that he would call when he was ready. Jason looked up and down the row of offices and back down at his cell phone. Seeing his confusion, I came down to greet him. I walked him over to a picnic bench nearby and we sat down.

He enjoyed being outdoors. He asked if he could smoke and I told him that if he smoked, I would likely get sick. He was kind of surprised by my response, but he obliged. I truly don't do well around cigarette smoke. I handed him his bag of food, which he ate ravenously. I sipped some water and ate a baguette.

Jason turned out to be a very intelligent young man, despite his mother's assertions otherwise. He was well-versed in many areas. He asked me a few personal questions, but nothing outlandish. He spoke about his upbringing and how he really had a good childhood with many friends and generally nice siblings. However, because of his lackadaisical approach to academics, he ended up failing many classes and then dropping out entirely after tenth grade. His mother tried homeschooling him, but they would butt heads often and the homeschooling stopped after a couple weeks. He began hanging around some guys he met from a nearby public school who shared a similar disdain for any sort of formal education.

In an act of defiance to his parents, Jason decided to get a couple of ear piercings. His mother went ballistic and sent him to talk to the family rabbi. The rabbi was very understanding and tried to reason with Jason's mother, but to no avail. The rabbi did establish a nice relationship with Jason, and Jason kept in contact with the rabbi from time to time. In the meantime, Jason was not in school and had no means of gainful employment. He began hanging out with drug users and attending raves and other parties where drugs and sexual promiscuity were rampant. Jason didn't believe in the use of hard drugs, especially after losing a couple friends to drugs. He did have some will to live. That was something that I would work with: his desire to live.

After Jason devoured his food, he informed me that he needed to leave soon. I asked him if we could meet the following week and he agreed. He again negotiated a food arrangement, which was fine since his parents were paying to keep him kosher. However, I requested that this time we meet in my office. He agreed and gave me a handshake, one which I was unfamiliar with. I asked him to teach me how to do that when we met next. I noticed a small awkward smile as he turned to go.

People want respect. I have also learned that young men like Jason feel great when they can teach an adult a thing or two. This happens frequently as my technological sophistication does not rival my psychological know-how. The point is that teens and young adults feel respected when they are asked for help. The problem is that parents don't necessarily appreciate the areas in which they can be very helpful. I see this often and wish parents could celebrate what their kids know how to do as opposed to focusing on what they don't *want* to do.

I made a brief call to Jason's father to inform him that Jason agreed to a third meeting. His father just said, "Thank you and good luck." I could tell he was checked out. I really felt bad for this father. He certainly was not on the same page as Jason's mother and seemed powerless to do anything.

I decided on a different tactic. I would get the most respected rabbi from the community to meet with the mother alone. I coordinated the following arrangement. The father would have an appointment with me at the same time the mother met with the rabbi. The mother agreed with this arrangement as she had frequently asked this rabbi questions in the area of Jewish law. This rabbi was also very familiar with the teen/young adult population, especially with this particular family.

Jason's father opened up more freely out of the presence of his wife, which is what I was hoping for. He was more open to unconventional tactics and was less concerned about Jason keeping kosher. His main concerns were how to keep the rest of the family intact and keeping Jason alive.

I made a follow-up appointment to meet with the rabbi to offer my impressions. The rabbi was very sympathetic to the cause and agreed that the mother would need to be spoken to alone while I worked with the father, mostly to validate his concerns. I explained that my role was to help Jason, and he thanked me for going out of the typical protocol of a therapist to assist the family.

My next appointment with Jason took place at my office. Jason wore somewhat respectable clothing, but that was not a requirement for his meeting with me. Jason launched into a tirade about his previous school and, of course, his mother, whom he blamed mostly for his current predicament. At one point, he looked at me and apologized for using so many curse words. I explained to him that although he would never hear any of those words coming from me, I would not judge him if he slipped up from time to time. Jason was clearly angry and did not want to return to his old lifestyle the way it was. He did admit that his current living situation could not last much longer, as he was getting sick of being used and ripped off from random people who frequented the apartment. I recommended that Jason try living at the home of an older couple, Mr. and Mrs. Goldberg, who had taken in kids in the past and had much success in dealing with them. I explained to Jason that although he would have some sense of autonomy at their home, he would have to play by their rules. This meant that he could not invite anyone over to the house without their consent. No drug or cigarette use in the house, no music without headphones, and a strict curfew of twelve midnight. A generous community donor, who was part of my "community team" and had a sincere interest in helping this population, agreed to pay the couple for food and other expenses.

Jason thought about his options and agreed to give it a try. The first week went without incident. However, Jason quickly learned that this couple meant business. They waited up one night, and Jason returned ten minutes late. They informed him that he would have to pack his bags in the morning for violating the curfew that night. Jason begged for another chance, but the couple did not budge. They had been through this before and knew how to play the game. Kids want rules. Kids want consistency. Their rules were not overly restrictive. But Jason messed up already. He called me up and told me he was getting kicked out.

I told Jason to meet me back in the office in the morning and we would talk about it. Jason came on time with a backpack, looking very upset. His anger was mostly with himself. I did not tell his parents that he had been kicked out of his new living quarters because I knew what the response would be. Besides, it would be totally counterintuitive given the nature of their relationship with each other and with Jason. Instead, I instructed Jason to do what I had done with other teens who had a similar arrangement with this couple. He was to write a handwritten apology without excuses. He was also to offer to do something extra that was not among the rules created by the Goldbergs. Jason said he would offer to mow their lawn every other week. I said I would propose the idea to the couple, but they had no obligation to take him back. The couple played right into the plan and said he would have to come to their house with me present and discuss what had happened.

The next evening, Jason and I went over to the couple's house. The ride over to the Goldbergs was a silent one by my choosing. I wanted to let Jason feel a little guilty for letting me down after I had found him a very nice place to live and for having messed up so soon. As we parked, Jason looked over at me. I shrugged my shoulders and gestured for him to get out.

We walked up to the door. The couple answered the door of their well-appointed home and gestured for us to sit down on the couch. Jason looked very nervous. Mr. Goldberg looked Jason directly in the eyes and said nothing. He also wanted to make Jason sweat a little before talking. Jason finally opened up by saying, "I'm sorry for violating curfew." Waiting for a response, he received none. He then handed over his handwritten apology that contained the offer to mow their lawn. Mr. Goldberg, a military man who was unfazed by wayward youth, motioned for Jason to get up and walk with him outside to the patio. There, I assume Mr. Goldberg read Jason the riot act because Jason came back with his head down in shame. Mr. Goldberg then came over to me and said, "We'll speak."

When we got back to the car, Jason said that Mr. Goldberg was not going to let him back because he could spot a con artist and was not convinced by Jason's crocodile tears, as he described them. I had seen Mr. Goldberg do this time and time again. He was the master—which was why I chose him in the first place.

Jason asked me what he should do. I told him that I would try to plead on his behalf. The rest of the ride was silent, and I could see that Jason was feeling really bad. Finally, he broke the silence and asked me why he always messed up. I explained how young people tend to be impulsive and feel invincible. He was realizing the harsh realities of the world and asked where he should stay that night while we figured something out. I called the rabbi who said he could stay the night with him. I thanked the rabbi and dropped Jason off. The rabbi welcomed him in and gave him something to eat before going off to give a class. The next morning, I called Jason and informed him that the Goldbergs would like to meet with him again.

The stern expression on the faces of the Goldbergs reinforced to Jason that they meant business. Prior to the meeting, I had instructed Jason to let the Goldbergs do the talking. Mr. Goldberg began. "Jason, we accepted you into our home under certain conditions. We are not young people. Our children are all grown up and live on their own. We do not need any extra people living among us. We accepted Dr. Lasson's offer as a courtesy because we have known him for quite some time. As much as you have let us down, you have also let down Dr. Lasson."

Mr. Goldberg let these words sink in. "After you left, we had the opportunity to discuss your situation with Dr. Lasson. He pleaded with us to give you another chance. I was not on board, for the record, but Mrs. Goldberg asked me to reconsider. I have thought about it, and I am willing to take you back. However, your curfew is now eleven instead of midnight. Not a minute later." Mr. Goldberg then took out a watch from his pocket and handed it to Jason. It was not an extremely expensive watch, but it was nicer than any watch Jason had ever owned.

Mr. Goldberg said to Jason, "If you love life, don't waste time, for time is what life is made up of."

"Do you know who said that?" asked Mr. Goldberg.

Jason shook his head.

"I didn't hear you. Did you say something?" said Mr. Goldberg in a louder tone.

"No, sir, I've never heard that quote," Jason said sheepishly.

"That was from Bruce Lee. Karate guy."

The name registered with Jason.

"Do you understand our rules, or do I have to get Bruce Lee to come here and drill them into you?"

Jason replied, "I understand."

"Do you want to live at our home?"

"Yes, sir."

"Good. I have a one-strike rule. Don't let Dr. Lasson down, but more importantly, don't let yourself down! I will see you later. Supper is at six. Sloppy Joe tonight, honey?"

"Yes dear," Mrs. Goldberg replied.

Jason looked at me. I looked back at Jason and assessed his reaction. It seemed obvious that he had never been spoken to this way. It was also clear that he had never seen a man communicate with his wife the way Mr. and Mrs. Goldberg communicated with each other.

As we drove away, Jason was mostly quiet and contemplative. He seemed lost in thought until he finally asked, "Have you really sent other people like me to live with them?"

"Absolutely!" I replied. "They are very good people who have raised very successful children. Mr. Goldberg will grow on you, if you allow him to."

"It's just kind of weird. I know I have to get away from my buddies. They aren't doing anything good for my life. My life basically sucks. I can't stand my mother and my father is a wimp. The Goldbergs are definitely different."

"Jason, your parents are good people who care about you. Otherwise, they would not have asked me to step in. They just might not have what you have needed from them…just yet."

"Well, I don't think they'll change. But I think I can get used to this family. Eleven o'clock is pretty early, but I see that he can't be played. And I don't want to go back to living with a bunch of freakin' potheads."

"That will be up to you, Jason."

Jason and I continued to meet weekly and sometimes twice a week. These sessions were refreshing for me personally. As I have gotten older, I find myself struggling to understand the teen/young adult culture. I always thought I had a pretty good grasp of how they operate. However, times have changed. Social influences are more difficult to reject and/or distance from. Teens seem to feel more emboldened to have a say in politics even though they do not follow the news. I don't even attempt to challenge their beliefs because after discussions with them, which are usually one-sided, they will ultimately come to the conclusion that they really don't understand what is happening but they are just echoing the sentiment they hear from bloggers or influencers. I wish I could record some of these conversations at times. I am usually very quiet and will just interject, "That's an interesting idea," from time to time. At the end of the "conversation," the teenager will usually admit that they do not really care about what they are saying. They just want to be heard and not be cut off mid-sentence. I firmly believe that if more adults would employ this tactic, they would see that the disagreements would be minimized.

Jason was articulate; I could foresee him becoming a public speaker at some point. For Jason, his parents were far too conservative and would express their views frequently rejecting any other opposing viewpoint. This does not sit well with most people Jason's age, and it certainly did not work for Jason. He also saw, as he began his teenage years, the hypocrisy in some of the things his parents preached and practiced. Jason could not find much hypocrisy in me because I hardly would interject a comment that had no basis. Instead, I would feed into his conversations by asking a question or by simply validating his feelings.

For the next several weeks, Jason maintained himself and did not break any rules. In fact, he enjoyed coming back earlier than his given curfew or simply not going out at all. He developed an adoration for Mrs. Goldberg and would spend hours just talking with her about life. He also asked her if he could help her cook and if she could teach him some of her basic culinary skills. Mrs. Goldberg also had an extensive collection of books, since she had been a literature major and taught classes at a local university. Jason developed a ravenous appetite for these books and would often fall asleep with a book on his stomach. Mrs. Goldberg suggested that Jason enroll at a community college after taking his GED exam. Jason jumped at the opportunity. Within a very short time, Jason received his GED and enrolled in an English and an economics course. Mrs. Goldberg would drop him off before class and he would take public transportation home. As it turned out, Jason aced both of those classes and quickly decided that he would continue his education at a four-year university. I approached my community team, which consisted of a few individuals from the Baltimore Jewish community, to help get Jason situated with a tuition arrangement to help pay for his schooling. They saw Jason's progress and agreed to help.

Jason also developed a relationship with Mr. Goldberg. He would mow the lawn and listen to Mr. Goldberg share stories from when he was young. Mr. Goldberg, in turn, would turn to Jason and ask for help with his computer and cell phone. Jason was happy to help. The arrangement was working out very well.

During our next session, Jason came in and sat down on the couch. He looked like he had not slept in a while. He was about to speak when he burst out in tears. After calming down, I asked Jason what happened. Between sniffles, Jason said that Mr. Goldberg had given him a hug the night before. I asked him how that made him feel. He said his parents had never given him a hug or told him that they loved him. He went on to tell me about Mrs. Goldberg. He said that she enjoyed cooking with him, and she even allowed him to make meals for their little family. He seemed lost in his thoughts, and he said he was surprised that he had become so emotional. I let him process that for a bit. He then updated me about his progress in his college classes (which were mostly online). I was very happy for Jason and asked him about his next steps.

"I don't want to go through life hating my parents. I want them to change, but I am realizing that maybe they can't, and I just have to accept stuff. They just seem so fake, and the Goldbergs are so real. There is no comparison. I think my dad would like me to lead a different kind of life, but he just follows my mom. He doesn't like arguments. I used to have these thoughts that my dad would shove my mom against the wall and scream at her at the top of his lungs. It sounds terrible, but I kind of wish that my father would be the tough guy like Mr. Goldberg—although Mr. Goldberg would never slam his wife against the wall. They have an amazing relationship."

"The kind you want to have one day?"

"Yes," said Jason. "They have such respect for each other, and they spend time with each other...like they really love each other." Jason sat there shaking his head ever so slightly, lost in thought.

"You really admire them."

"What is not to admire? They literally turned my life around. Like legit."

"Where does that leave your parents?" I asked.

"Who cares? I'm in a good place now. And it's not because of my pathetic parents."

"I understand that you feel resentful toward your parents, and it seems like you've found a nice replacement for them." I let those words linger for just a moment. "But Jason," I continued, "you have a set of biological parents and siblings who care deeply for you. You may not like how they parented you, but they will always be the parents who gave you one important thing: your life."

"I see what you're saying, Doc. What are you suggesting I do?"

"I think you need to make peace with them and find a way to coexist."

"Are you suggesting that I go live with them? No way!"

"I am only suggesting that you try to accept them for who they are and look at their positive qualities. They care about you and have gone through many hours and dollars to try to get you back. How about if you start with just getting together for a meal? You can still live with the Goldbergs for now, but that arrangement has to end at some point."

"Then what?" Jason asked.

"Then…you either go back home or you find an apartment to live in," I offered.

"Lemme think about it," Jason countered.

"Fair enough."

At this point, I wanted to strike a chord about the importance of family. When one child rebels against their parents, the siblings become collateral damage.

"Jason, you will always have admiration for what the Goldbergs have done for you. But you have brothers and sisters as well who worry about you and want you to be part of their lives."

Jason sat there silent. It looked like he was about to shed a tear. I got up and said, "You think about it. I'm here to help if you need me."

I let Jason sit there with his thoughts while he waited for his ride.

On my way home, I thought about how to get Jason's parents to do what went against their religious fibers. In the past, I had employed the assistance of the rabbi and felt that I should again contact him due to his familiarity with Jason and his family. I contacted the rabbi, and he was more than willing to assist. I explained to him that he would be sort of a co-therapist to help speak to the parents.

We set up a time for Jason, his parents, the rabbi, and me to meet at the home of the rabbi. I was unsure how it would play out, but I knew the rabbi to be very delicate when dealing with these matters. When all were assembled in the rabbi's living room, the rabbi opened up by discussing how Jason was improving and the goal for our meeting was mutual acceptance. I was therefore quite surprised when the rabbi came down very hard on the parents. He punctuated his speech with multiple biblical and Talmudic references. When he finished his little speech, he began to cry.

You would have to know this rabbi to understand how genuine a man he is. It was his tears, though, that changed the entire course of the session. He pleaded for Mom and Dad to make changes that would allow Jason to feel accepted by them. He also pleaded with Jason to allow his parents the time to make these changes. He also informed Jason that his parents were bound to slip up from time to time and say the wrong things, but he insisted that it was coming from a place of love. He then asked Jason to step out of the room so he could speak with his parents and me privately. When Jason left the house, the rabbi told Jason's father that he must step up to the plate and that he would be checking in with him from time to time to make sure that he was taking a more active role in Jason's life. This meant encouraging Jason with his college pursuits and taking Jason out to spend time together. I was extremely impressed with the rabbi's ability to facilitate a change just by showing how much he cared.

Over the next few weeks, there was a visible change in Jason's demeanor. He seemed calmer than ever before. He began spending more time at his parents' home for Shabbat meals. He went out with his father every Sunday and agreed not to discuss anything related to religion. This was becoming easier for Dad as he became very interested in what Jason was studying. Jason had learned to accept his mother and could deal with her for small periods of time. He began to reconnect with his siblings in a more meaningful way. He would take his siblings out to places (that were mutually agreed upon by me and his parents), and they were overjoyed to have their big brother back in their lives. Jason confided in me that he really had missed his siblings and promised to be a positive role model for them. He was respectful of the rules that his parents had in the home, and they understood that what Jason did outside of the home was up to him.

In my work with children having difficulties with their parents, I do not typically see change happen so quickly. The intervention of my rabbi/co-therapist and the help of the wonderful Goldberg family certainly helped hasten the improvements in the family's unity. However, I came to the realization that children want others to set the bar much higher than what they are usually accustomed to. They want others to believe in their capabilities and give them the wings to soar. The cliché, "It takes a village," could not have been more appropriate in Jason's case as it took many involved players to facilitate his recovery.

Jason's story is also one of resilience. There were many factors that placed Jason in the at-risk category for future delinquency and possible criminal behavior. A low support system from home, low self-esteem, poor choices in friends—those factors were replaced through the interventions during Jason's journey back to a productive and functional life.

Professor Emmy Werner describes this sense of resilience in many of her scholarly works on the topic and identifies some of these variables that help children and young adults learn to deal with adversity during the shifting balances at each developmental stage. She also identifies gender and protective issues that determine the extent of how resilient people become despite high risk factors. In Jason's case, being a male, which is commonly a demographic associated with resilience, along with many strong attributes that eventually led him back to his sense of self, proved critical in his recovery and helping this therapist find Jason again.

A LETTER TO
NEXT-GENERATION
THERAPISTS

Dear Future Therapist,

You have just read my personal account of what it is like to be a therapist in this day and age. Therapy has certainly evolved since I began in 2000. Twenty-two years and so many advancements. My motivation to become a mental health professional was probably very similar to yours. I wanted to help people and impact their lives in a positive way. Therapy is a glorious profession.

I want to focus on the "profession" aspect of that sentence for a moment. A profession is defined by the Oxford Dictionary as "a paid occupation, especially one that involves prolonged training and a formal qualification." This definition means you are in it to make money. Always remember that. It is not a negative quality to want to earn a living. We all have to survive. This idea of making money from the work we do often gets lost when we are starting out in graduate school and want to help as many people as possible. But we need to earn a living, and we deserve to earn a living from the work we do. A friend of mine often sends me cases from the law firm where he works. He once asked me why I don't charge more. Coming from a paralegal, I was tempted to dismiss the comment, but I thought about it and realized he was right. For years, I had not been adequately compensated for the services I provided. I took his advice seriously and adjusted my rates to match the amount that I deserve based on my education, years of experience, and expertise in the area. Secondly, a profession involves "prolonged training." Your training never ends! You will always be learning something new. You are required by legal and ethical standards to remain relevant and up to date. After you graduate, you will be required to continue your professional training by attending conferences and workshops.

You are always practicing. I always found the term private practice interesting. When Dr. Smith tells me that at age eighty, he has been in private practice throughout his entire career, I have to wonder, why are you still "practicing"? When I think of practicing, to me it means that I am preparing for the real thing. If I am still practicing at eighty, does that mean I have never experienced the real thing?

This leads me to another important point. There is no approach that will work with every client you encounter. No one in their right mind would ever tell you (at least I would hope not) that they have a one-hundred percent success rate as a therapist. You will have clients who will terminate therapy unexpectedly. You will have clients that will write negative reviews about you. You will have clients who will hurt your feelings. Yes, it is true. We are all humans, and we all have feelings. I have had clients who said, "I thought you would be able to help me," or "You are supposed to have the answers." How do therapists walk away from those hurtful comments? We feel hurt and we sometimes obsess about what we did wrong or could have done better. (We are not flower delivery people or Amazon drivers who almost universally feel great because people are always happy to receive flowers and packages.)

There is no one modality that fits all. To this day I meet therapists who will try to convince me that I should take training in a certain modality. Why are they trying to convert me? I am always hearing about new advances from young therapists who say, "You absolutely *have* to take this training. It will be a game changer." When I hear those words "you have to," I automatically assume that this person has been brainwashed. This leads to my next piece of advice.

We live in a very divisive world where people of different affiliations will not speak to one another peacefully. It breaks up families, work relationships, and our ability to have civil conversations where we listen to someone's opinion, contemplate it, and make a choice that suits us best. As a religious person, I refrain from engaging in certain conversations because it is easier to be under the radar. What would it cost me if I spoke my mind? Nowadays, the costs are tremendous. Whatever I say in written or spoken form can be used against me. Does that mean I don't have opinions about things? Absolutely not! I choose not to speak because I don't like to ruffle feathers with people who I will probably never interact with again. If I am at a coffee shop and someone strikes up a conversation with me, I will typically nod my head, smile from time to time, and validate what they are saying, no matter how asinine they sound.

Another piece of advice. Avoid the temptation to write an "Ask the Shrink" column. I have refused and continue to refuse offers to write columns that ask me, as a therapist, to comment on a particular topic. I typically don't know someone until I have at least ten sessions with that person. How is it possible to answer a question from someone I don't know at all? I don't know how these therapists do it. Maybe they just have a sixth sense and can figure out every nuance of a family dynamic from a two-sentence question. But my advice is—as I've said for many years—train yourself to say, "I don't know" or "I would not be able to answer that question until I hear the whole story."

On my next point I will tread lightly because I'm dealing with two subjects that sometimes seem quite heavy: religion and politics. Religion and politics are no longer off limits, but they have limits. Let's talk about religion first. If you happen to be religious, the field of psychology might present some dilemmas that you will have to consider. Many of my religious colleagues have felt somewhat conflicted in recent years. The conflict occurs not necessarily with the clients. The conflict usually manifests with my colleagues and the state and national boards that govern our field. We are supposed to be culturally sensitive and competent. One area of cultural insensitivity comes to light when colleagues make assumptions about us because of our religious beliefs and worldviews. I would venture to say they are microaggressions against religious people. One of my Muslim colleagues stated that he had an issue with a non-religious colleague who told him that his religious beliefs made him "close minded" toward the treatment of certain populations. Another experience I personally had was with a client who shared that her non-religious therapist suggested that her depression and anxiety stemmed directly from her religious practices. She was encouraged by this therapist to live freely and promiscuously and practice her faith as much or as little as she wanted. This caused her more anxiety and guilt than she had already been experiencing. A sort of bias against religious therapists is more common than you may think. The movie industry has fed the perception of religious people as cultish, outdated, restrictive, and abusive. This negative view of religion challenges mental health professionals who tend to be more progressive than their religious counterparts, many with good intentions but who are conflicted when it comes to dealing with specific mental health issues that interface with religion.

And now...to a subject I know very little about, but the truth is that you are not really living in this world if you are not exposed to political conversations. So I feel compelled to make mention of how politics affects the ability to reach and help clients. It begins with what you put into your office—literally and figuratively. If you are of a certain political affiliation and your books or tchotchkes convey your political mindset, it can cause some friction or create barriers between you and your client. So I suggest a neutral environment and attitude that sidesteps potential issues. My advice is to keep politics out of therapy. Period.

I continue to meet students of psychology and psychologists just beginning their career who are cheerful and full of life. They aspire to help people and make a difference. I applaud you. As I mentioned in the beginning of this letter, therapy is in fact a glorious profession. As illustrated in my first book, *The Guilt Trap*, and this book that you have just read, there are ups and downs. There are days you will feel invigorated. There will be other times when you will question if you are doing the right thing. That's okay. What's not okay is to keep it all to yourself. Share how you feel about a situation with a colleague, and not just any colleague. Try to talk to a colleague who can offer a different perspective from yours, not someone who will validate your every word and make you feel like you are doing everything right. I am reminded of a man who was eulogizing his mother. When his mother was diagnosed with ovarian cancer, she asked her son to take her to another doctor for a second opinion. So, he took her for a second opinion. The next doctor gave the same grim diagnosis and prognosis. She again asked her son to take her for a second opinion. The son said, "Mom, I took you to a second doctor, and he also said you have ovarian cancer." She replied, "That is correct. He did say that. But that was the same opinion as the first doctor. I want a second opinion—one that's different from ovarian cancer!"

Get a different opinion, and not one that confirms your deeply embedded beliefs. Psychology is often referred to as pseudoscience. It is not a hard science like math. People are complex and just when you think you are headed in the right direction, your client inevitably surprises you. Be flexible.

I wish you the best of luck as you pursue this glorious profession. Be aware of the challenges, your personal biases, and your need to take a break from time to time. May you enjoy decades of fulfillment from your good work.

Best wishes,
Dr. Jonathan Lasson
April 27, 2022

ACKNOWLEDGMENTS

When a project of mine is nearing its completion, I tend to get emotional. I am truly humbled to see my second book come to fruition. The process can feel somewhat long at times. And writing during a global pandemic only added to that. I would say that COVID-19 both helped and hindered the process.

The pandemic helped me and probably many others reset and learn to adapt. Part of that adaptation was working from home. Finding a space to write should not have to be a problem. However, a little background noise helps motivate and inform my writing. For me, writing a book of psychotherapy tales requires distraction. Seeing a variety of people at a coffee shop inspires me to apply different characteristics to the actual clients I have served over the years in order to help disguise their identities. So when coffee shops closed their doors, finding a place to write at home was not easy. It was just too quiet. When things began opening up, I set myself into high gear. I was working on two written projects at the same time. The one that you are reading right now and one which will require a little more time and effort as it involves using multiple languages.

The hindering factors include all the work that goes into completing any book. There is the editing. And more editing. And more editing. Plus, there is a supply chain issue that is slowing down production in the publishing industry. There has been a shift from traditional publishing to self-publishing, which has caused an influx of writers like myself to try to get their books out into the market in short order.

Family events and challenges have also encompassed much of the last year. Having three grandchildren in a little over a year has been life-altering. I love them so much and am grateful for every moment I get to spend with them. I am so proud of my children for all they do. We are constantly adapting to these wonderful additions to our family. Life is all about adaptation.

Having an ailing family member during a pandemic has impacted many people in real and meaningful ways. Watching my mother decline so rapidly certainly impacted me. My mother had been such a constant in our family. In April of 2021, she was still an active person, driving and cooking and visiting with people. Then she had a fall and things changed. Her passing in December of 2021 put me in an emotional fog, just as I was completing my final chapter. Again, I had to adapt.

I would say I get my work ethic from my father. Even as he approaches his mid-eighties, my father is still working full time as a clinical psychologist and giving and attending courses in Jewish law, psychology, and biblical thought. I am forever thankful for his support and what he has taught me about work ethic and mental health.

When I was writing my first book, *The Guilt Trap*, in 2017, I discovered Victoria Lasin of VL Editing. Victoria worked with my short timeline and proved to be an extremely valuable asset to my work, and I am forever grateful. Victoria's insights, her ability to help me drive home a point, and her appreciation of my humor have made this project something other than work. It has been a joy.

Ruth Schwartz, aka The Wonderlady, is the dynamic force who once again helped me with my second birth, the book you are looking at. Ruth is very knowledgeable and confident about the whole publishing process, as well as an accomplished writer herself. I am so happy to have the opportunity to benefit from her expertise.

Many colleagues and supervisors have been instrumental in the work I do. I regularly bounce ideas off these colleagues who will offer advice and often ask, "You did that with that client?" It is said that sometimes you learn what to do by watching others and learning what *not* to do. This has certainly enhanced my career. As I tell my kids and students, your best teacher is your last mistake. I am certainly not flawless, but I have the ability to know when I am wrong and admit my mistakes. I thank my religion and my conscience for this. As a religious Jew, I have benefitted from the advice of many rabbis who have assisted me in looking at many psychological issues through a biblical lens. This is the perspective that guides much of my practice for most of my Jewish clients experiencing existential issues.

Recently, I joined a magnificent group of clinicians. We share cases with each other and in a supportive, nonjudgmental environment. The group, led by Dr. Yehuda Bergman, has opened my eyes to new and very creative approaches for working with challenging clients. Clients and therapists can often reach a therapeutic stalemate, and this group has enabled all of us to be more creative.

I mentioned my children before. Although I typically do not involve my children in my work, they are very supportive of me. I want to thank Tehilla, Dovid, Meir, Akiva, Tamar, and Shalva for their support and the fun times we share together, which keep me grounded as a family man. Now I have one son-in-law and two daughters-in-law whom I love like my own children. Thank you to Daniel, Arielle, and Rivka for enhancing my life and for all you do for our family. I would also like to give a shout out to my youngest daughter Shalva who was instrumental in the design of the covers of both my books, the first of which won an award for best nonfiction cover in August 2017. She was only eight years old at the time, but I am continually amazed by her out-of-the-box creativity and artistic talents—which have helped readers "judge the book by its cover."

One of the best decisions in my life came almost thirty years ago when I married Chaya. Chaya has an endless amount of energy, which enables her to do so much work on behalf of the community as a director of hospice and palliative care. As busy as she is, she still manages to put delicious home-cooked suppers on the table every night, a family ritual we all cherish. As the song goes, "We can spend all our time making money or we can spend all our money making time." Chaya always chooses the latter and values the importance of quality time with our children and grandchildren.

Lastly, I would like to thank God. To say "lastly" doesn't do justice to God, the one who has guided me throughout my life and is ever present in all decisions I make. However, we have a dictum in Talmudic literature that says the last one is the most precious. Indeed, I would not have anything without the graciousness of the one above.

Made in the USA
Middletown, DE
27 August 2022

72461468R00126